ILLUMINATING UNITY

Illuminating Unity

Four Perspectives on Dei Verbum*'s "One Table of the Word of God and the Body of Christ"*

Rhodora E. Beaton

M G

A Michael Glazier Book

LITURGICAL PRESS
Collegeville, Minnesota

www.litpress.org

A Michael Glazier Book published by Liturgical Press

Jodi Hendrickson. Illustration by Frank Kacmarcik, OblSB.

1 2 3 4 5 6 7 8 9

Library of Congress Cataloging-in-Publication Data

Beaton, Rhodora E.

Illuminating unity : four perspectives on Dei Verbum's "one table of the word of God and the body of Christ" / Rhodora E. Beaton.

pages cm

"A Michael Glazier book."

ISBN 978-0-8146-8056-8 — ISBN 978-0-8146-8057-5 (ebook)

1. Bible—Liturgical use. 2. Catholic Church—Liturgy. 3. Sermons. 4. Word of God (Christian theology) 5. Revelation—Catholic Church. I. Title.

BX1970.B38 2014
264'.02—dc23 2014016138

Contents

Acknowledgments

I am deeply grateful to the many people and institutions who have supported my work on this project. First, my thanks go to my graduate school mentors, Cathy Hilkert, Bob Krieg, and Nathan Mitchell. This project finds its roots in questions that I have been thinking about for nearly a decade. I am grateful for your research, example, support, and encouragement.

This project was exhilarating in part because it pushed me into new areas of research. Colleagues Kimberly Baker and Jack Conroy were especially generous in sharing their respective expertise in the fields of Augustine and Philo studies. Thank you for e-mails, articles, insights, and citations! Any errors are, of course, entirely my own. Thanks go also to Joyce Slaughter, for stimulating interreligious conversations about the sacramentality of the word of God, and to the members of the NAAL Liturgical Language seminar, who offered generous feedback on many facets of this project.

I am grateful for the institutional support that I received from St. Catherine University, in the form of course release time, and from the Wabash Center for Teaching and Learning in Theology and Religion, in the form of a summer fellowship. The time provided for thinking and writing was invaluable. I am also very grateful to everyone at Liturgical Press both for the initial encouragement and for the careful and professional editorial process.

Finally, thanks are due to the family members who have nourished my theological imagination and supported me along the way. I am grateful to Rod and Mary Ann Beaton; Elizabeth Ryan and Patrick Ryan; Terra Beaton; Roderick, Michelle, Owen, and Anna Beaton; and always, and especially, to Todd Hanneken.

Introduction

Illuminating Unity

On October 11, 1962, having attended the opening liturgy of the Second Vatican Council, French Dominican theologian Yves Congar reflected on the experience in his personal journal. He described the entrance of the bishops, the clapping of the crowd, and the singing of the *Veni Creator* by Pope John XXIII and the Sistine Choir. Commenting on the lack of intentional liturgical participation among the assembly, he observed that "the liturgical movement ha[d] not yet reached the Roman Curia."[1] In addition to the lack of what *Sacrosanctum Concilium* would later call "full, conscious, and active" participation (SC 14),[2] Congar's observations also include his lament that,

> there is nothing here except for the eye and the musical ear: No liturgy of the Word. No spiritual word. I know that in a few minutes a Bible will be placed on a throne in order to preside over the Council. BUT WILL IT SPEAK? Will it be listened to? Will there be a moment for the Word of God?[3]

1. Yves Congar, *My Journal of the Council*, trans. Mary John Ronayne and Mary Cecily Boulding (Collegeville, MN: Liturgical Press, 2012), 56.

2. All excerpts from the documents of Vatican II in this book are taken from *Vatican Council II: The Basic Sixteen Documents; Constitutions, Decrees, Declarations*, ed. Austin Flannery (Collegeville, MN: Liturgical Press, 2014).

3. Congar, *My Journal of the Council*, 87.

Congar's reflections illustrate the ritual enthronement of the gospels at the beginning of each congregation of the council as well as the attention to beauty, visible and musical, which was well developed in the Catholic sacramental tradition. His point, however, highlights that which was missing. The biblical word of God, while venerated, was "seen and not heard," even in the elaborate liturgy celebrated to open the council.

Building on the great progress made by the liturgical movement in the years prior to and following the Second Vatican Council, efforts to find "a moment for the Word of God" in Catholic liturgical practice continue. In many parishes, the training of lectors has become a priority. In some dioceses, preaching workshops are offered for priests and deacons who wish to improve their homiletic capabilities. Yet Congar's "moment" for the word of God has not yet been fully achieved in Catholic liturgical celebration. In his first Apostolic Exhortation, *Evangelii Gaudium*, Pope Francis illustrated this struggle in his discussion of the significance of the homily in the liturgy. He writes, "We know that the faithful attach great importance to [the homily], and that both they and their ordained ministers suffer because of homilies: the laity from having to listen to them and the clergy from having to preach them! It is sad that this is the case."[4] The pope's wry acknowledgment of this problem points to the challenges that Catholics continue to face in celebrating a liturgy in which the Liturgy of the Word, including the preaching, is not merely regarded as "the unavoidable preparation for the sacrament"[5] but is understood as inherent to the liturgical celebration as a whole.

In order to find a "moment" for the word of God and to develop the theological and liturgical infrastructure to support its continued recognition and reception, a new approach to the theological consideration of the relationship between word and sacrament is needed. This approach must be grounded in the liturgy, but avoid the hierarchical dualism which the traditional pairing of Liturgy of the Word and Liturgy of the Eucharist sets up. Despite recent work to highlight the connections between what *Sacrosanctum Concilium* calls these "two parts" of the liturgy, which "are so closely connected with each other that they form but one single act of worship" (SC 56), centuries of Catholic emphasis on the Liturgy of

4. Francis, "*Evangelii Gaudium*," *Origins* 43, no. 27–28 (2013): 135.

5. Karl Rahner, "The Word and the Eucharist," in *Theological Investigations 4* (New York: Crossroad, 1982), 257.

the Eucharist and Protestant emphasis on the Liturgy of the Word have set up a dualistic, and in some cases polemical, dynamic. A new model, however, is suggested in the metaphorical language of *Dei Verbum*, which reminds the faithful that their spiritual nourishment, the Bread of Life, is offered to them "from the one table of the word of God and Body of Christ" (DV 21). The image of this one table emphasizes the inherent unity of the liturgy and invites nondualistic theological reflection from a variety of perspectives. In an effort to reach a deeper understanding of the word of God, the body of Christ, and the unity of the liturgical celebration, we will consider the metaphor of the one table from four different perspectives: biblical prophecy, pneumatology, language, and sacramentality. Each perspective will draw from the depth and breadth of the theological tradition, highlighting areas of theological intersection.

While recognition of the unity of word and table is itself far from innovative—both Augustine of Hippo and Thomas Aquinas, among others, recognized it—the realization of this unity in theological and pastoral practice has been difficult to achieve in recent centuries.[6] Modern-day efforts to reflect this unity in Catholic liturgical practices began with the work of theologians such as Otto Semmelroth, Karl Rahner, and Edward Schillebeeckx prior to the council. Each of these theologians wrote about the close relationship between word and sacrament, and the significance of the revelatory word of God in the liturgical context.

Semmelroth's early argument in *The Preaching Word* illustrates the challenges any Catholic theologian faced in discussing the efficacy of the word of God prior to the Second Vatican Council. In 1962 Semmelroth wrote,

> the assertion that the word of God, in distinction from the sacraments, is always without any efficacy for the imparting of grace is just as unacceptable as the assertion that wherever we find mention of the word of God, we are confronted with a mystery in which God imparts himself and his grace fully and unequivocally.[7]

6. For a detailed examination of sacramental approaches to the word of God in the classical, Reformation, and modern-day eras, see my *Embodied Words, Spoken Signs: Sacramentality and the Word in Rahner and Chauvet*, Emerging Scholars Series (Minneapolis, MN: Fortress, 2014).

7. Otto Semmelroth, *The Preaching Word: On the Theology of Proclamation* (New York: Herder and Herder, 1965), 13.

Here Semmelroth argues simply for the possibility of the efficacy of the word of God, offered to humanity in a context distinct, although never entirely separated, from ritual sacramental words such as the words of institution. Semmelroth does not hesitate to acknowledge that such instances of the word of God—preaching or the proclamation of the Scriptures, for example—may be somewhat deficient in comparison with the ritual words. He argues simply for the *possibility* of the imparting of grace through the preached or proclaimed word, concluding that the most efficacious preaching is that which is most closely connected to the sacrament.[8] Semmelroth's approach values the biblical word of God to the degree that it is related to the sacraments; this approach continues to ground much subsequent Roman Catholic work on the topic.

Semmelroth's work on the potential efficacy of preaching can be read in relation to the work of Karl Rahner and Edward Schillebeeckx, who also worked to revive a Roman Catholic theology of the word in the mid-twentieth century. Rahner's *logos* Christology grounds his understanding of liturgy and the sacraments in the theory of God's self-expression through the logos of God, which human beings are uniquely equipped to receive.[9] Even as God expresses who God is in the logos, humans behave similarly when they speak the "primordial words"[10] of poets to express the depths of what it means to be human. Arguing that the most potent of these words are found in the eucharistic words of institution, Rahner also acknowledges degrees of efficacy which may be found in other forms of human speech, including preaching and promises. Rahner's theology of the word suggests not only that preaching and proclamation can be efficacious experiences of the word of God but also that degrees of this efficacy can be found in the words of poets, lovers, and all human being who speak from the depths of their experience.

In the same decade, Edward Schillebeeckx expanded Catholic thinking on the sacraments in a manner which would pave the way for emerging sacramental theologies of the word. Schillebeeckx's understanding of the

8. Ibid., 244.

9. Karl Rahner, *Foundations of Christian Faith: An Introduction to the Idea of Christianity*, trans. William V. Dych (New York: Crossroad, 1997).

10. Karl Rahner, "Priest and Poet," in *Theological Investigations 3* (New York: Crossroad, 1967), 296.

sacraments as "encounters"[11] between God and humanity suggests an image of divine-human dialogue, which takes place through the exchange of words and symbols. Broadening the theological focus from the seven ritual sacraments, Schillebeeckx successfully argued that Christ could be understood as the "primordial sacrament"[12] and that the church itself be regarded as a kind of sacrament. This broad understanding of sacrament, which was reflected in both *Sacrosanctum Concilium* and *Lumen Gentium*, would help to ground the late twentieth-century interest in sacramentality, the recognition that all created reality has the potential to mediate the presence of God. It is within the theological understanding of sacramentality that many twentieth- and twenty-first-century Roman Catholic liturgical theologies of the word would find a home.

These Roman Catholic efforts to develop a sacramental theology of the word emerged in the context of the liturgical movement, the ecumenical movement, and the revival of Catholic biblical scholarship, which began with Pius XII's encyclical *Divino Afflante Spiritu*. The convergence of these movements became especially clear in the summer of 1963, which witnessed the first intersession of Vatican II, the World Council of Churches' Fourth World Conference on Faith and Order in Montreal, Canada, and several Protestant denominational meetings to which Roman Catholic observers were invited.[13] The Faith and Order meeting, which took up ecumenically significant topics such as worship and the relationship between Scripture and tradition, was particularly important. At the same time, Catholics, grieving the loss of John XXIII, were preparing for the second session of the Second Vatican Council to open under the leadership of Paul VI. This second session, which would conclude with the promulgation of the Constitution on the Sacred Liturgy, also preceded a particularly fruitful period of work during the spring of 1964 on the *schema* on divine revelation. With a few individuals attending both the

11. Edward Schillebeeckx, *Christ the Sacrament of the Encounter with God*, 1963 ed. (Franklin, WI: Sheed and Ward, 1999), 13–45.

12. Ibid., 13–20.

13. Jan Grootaers, "Ebb and Flow Between Two Seasons," in *The Formation of the Council's Identity First Period and Intersession October 1962–September 1963*, ed. Guiseppe Alberigo and Joseph A. Komonchak, History of Vatican II, vol. 2 (Maryknoll, NY: Orbis Books, 1997), 535–46.

Faith and Order meeting and the Second Vatican Council,[14] both the World Council of Churches and the Catholic Church spoke seriously about the need for liturgical unity as a prerequisite for doctrinal unity among the Christian churches. Each group also took up topics more commonly of concern to the other, with the WCC's Faith and Order Commission hearing reports on the relationship between Scripture and tradition, and with the Catholic Church discussing the significance of the word of God offered to humanity in the Scriptures.[15]

The significance of liturgical practice as a step toward ecumenical unity was of central concern at both meetings. In the "Foreword" to the compiled reports of the Theological Commission on Worship, Patrick Rodger observed that "it is surely in the realm of worship that the paradox of Christian unity and disunity can be most plainly seen." He went on to state that on the one hand, "when we 'go to the altar of God' a good many of the questions and arguments with which we entered are stilled . . . on the other hand, it is also notorious that it is in matters of worship . . . that the conservatism of Christian people operates most strongly against change, and therefore against that renewal by the Holy Spirit which . . . is agreed . . . to be the pre-requisite of unity."[16] Rodger's acknowledgment points to one of the fundamental challenges of the convergence of the ecumenical and liturgical movements. On the one hand, it is in the liturgical encounter with God that we are most able to set technical matters of doctrine aside. On the other hand, as the old axiom *lex orandi, lex credendi* reminds us, it is in the ingrained habits of prayer and ritual practice that Christians find and nurture their particular identities as Christians. The risk of changing these habits seems, perhaps rightly, very

14. These included Johannes Willebrands, Secretary for the Vatican's Secretariat for Christian Unity, and Lukas Vischer of the World Council of Churches' Faith and Order Commission.

15. As Gregory Baum would put it in an August 1963 article in *Commonweal*, "We have here undoubtedly an area of ecumenical triumph. Catholics and Protestants have recognized that their understanding of tradition and its relation to the Scriptures has largely been colored by polemical preoccupations." Gregory Baum, "A Broadening of the Base: Montreal: Faith and Order," *The Commonweal* 78, no. 19 (1963): 510.

16. Patrick C. Rodger, and Regin Prenter, J. Russell Chandran, Joseph Sittler, *Paper 39. Report of the Theological Commission on Worship* (Geneva: World Council of Churches, Commission on Faith and Order, 1963).

great. Liturgical change, therefore, is often a slow and difficult process. Despite these difficulties, both the Faith and Order Commission and the Second Vatican Council continued to pursue the dual goals of liturgical reform and liturgical unity. The first paragraph of *Sacrosanctum Concilium*, which states among its goals the explicit intention "to encourage whatever can promote the union of all who believe in Christ," concludes by noting that "accordingly [the council] sees particularly cogent reasons for undertaking the reform and promotion of the liturgy" (SC 1). Here, as with the Faith and Order Commission, liturgical reforms were undertaken with the goal of Christian unity in mind.

While the hopes for unity were of great significance, it was also the case that in their official documents, both Catholics and Protestants were acknowledging the inadequacy of their current forms of worship. The Faith and Order Commission of the World Council of Churches observed "that the liturgical forms and language of the churches, including that of preaching, are everywhere in need of transformation . . . [adding that these liturgical] traditions are inadequate for the current mission of the church."[17] *Sacrosanctum Concilium* stated similarly that "it is the wish of the church to undertake a careful general reform of the liturgy in order that the Christian people may be more certain to derive an abundance of graces from it" (SC 21). Liturgical reforms across denominations were thus undertaken, sometimes—as in the case of the International Consultation on Common Texts, a reform in which ICEL participated—in direct ecumenical collaboration.[18] A renewal of preaching and increased participation on the parts of the faithful were significant results of these reforms.

Such ecumenical efforts to promote Christian unity through liturgical reform occurred in tandem with discussions of doctrinal and cultural issues which had separated Protestants and Catholics since the Reformation. Primary among these in 1963 were the doctrinal issues surrounding the relationship between Scripture and tradition, which had played out

17. Ibid., 69.

18. Horace T. Allen, "Common Lectionary and Protestant Hymnody: Unity at the Table of the Word—Liturgical and Ecumnical Bookends," in *Liturgical Renewal as a Way to Christian Unity*, ed. James F. Puglisi (Collegeville, MN: Liturgical Press, 2005), 63.

in the liturgical practices of Catholics and Protestants since the sixteenth century. Addressing these difficulties directly, the Faith and Order Commission of the World Council of Churches began its discussion on the topic of tradition in the summer of 1963. Distinguishing between tradition (lowercase, singular), which designates "the traditionary process operating in human history and society,"[19] traditions (lowercase, plural), which denote the different types of denominational traditions, including liturgical traditions,[20] and *the* Tradition (capitalized, singular), which is "of divine origination," and is "the referent to which the plural traditions refer if they can rightly be classed as mutually related to each other,"[21] the European report on tradition also addressed the neuralgic issue of the relationship between Scripture and tradition, concluding that all Christians exist "by the Tradition of the Gospel testified in Scripture."[22] Emphasizing the connection between liturgy and doctrine, the commission clarified that this tradition is "actualized in the preaching of the Word, in the administration of the sacraments and worship" as well as in "theology, missionary work, and the overall life of the church."[23] As the European report on worship put it, "thus both in the Gospel proclaimed and in the sacrament performed there is present one and the same God. . . . But it is proper to say that Christ is present in different modes."[24] This understanding of the presence of God, experienced by humanity in Gospel and sacrament, reflects the liturgical realization of the convergence in doctrinal understanding of the relationship between Scripture and tradition.

19. World Council of Churches, *The Report of the Theological Commission on Tradition and Traditions: Fourth World Conference on Faith and Order, Montreal, Canada, 12–26 July, 1963*, Faith and Order Paper no. 40 (Geneva: World Council of Churches, Faith and Order Commission, 1963), 16.

20. Ibid., 17.

21. Ibid.

22. Ibid.

23. Ibid.

24. Günther Gassmann, *Documentary History of Faith and Order, 1963–1993*, Faith and Order Paper no. 159 (Geneva: WCC Publications, 1993), 12. The report concluded that "it is not profitable to compare the intensity of the various modes of his presence, and this error has been at the root of many past controversies."

In a parallel discussion, the Second Vatican Council debated what the Council of Trent and the First Vatican Council had referred to as supernatural revelation offered "in written books and in unwritten traditions."[25] After a total of four drafts, *Dei Verbum*, the Constitution on Divine Revelation, described Scripture and tradition as "the single sacred deposit of the word of God which is entrusted to the church," concluding that with the magisterium of the church, they "are so connected and associated that one of them cannot stand without the others. Working together, each in its own way under the action of the one Holy Spirit, they all contribute effectively to the salvation of souls" (DV 10). *Dei Verbum*, in continuity with *Sacrosanctum Concilium*,[26] likewise attended to the significance of the liturgy, emphasizing the need for scriptural preaching (DV 21, 23–25) and suggesting the possibility of ecumenical translation projects (DV 22). Turning, as the World Council of Churches discussion did, to the topic of the presence of Christ in the liturgy, the Second Vatican Council also expressed an expanded understanding of God's presence in the liturgy, explaining that

> Christ is always present in his church, especially in liturgical celebrations. He is present in the sacrifice of the Mass, both in the person of his minister . . . and most of all in the eucharistic species. By his power he is present in the sacraments so that when anyone baptizes it is really Christ himself who baptizes. He is present in his word, since it is he himself who speaks when the holy scriptures are read in church. Lastly he is present, when the church prays and sings." (SC 7)

This famous fourfold expression of the presence of Christ in the liturgy opened the doors for a greater respect for the proclamation and preaching of the word in Catholic liturgical practice, as well as for the full, conscious, active participation of the laity (SC 14) in the church's communal prayer and song. As was the case with the Faith and Order reports, the doctrinal consideration of the relationship between Scripture and tradition carried

25. See "Canons and Decrees of the Council of Trent," in *Decrees of the Ecumenical Councils*, ed. Norman P. Tanner, vol. 2 (Washington, DC: Georgetown University Press, 1990), 663–64; and "Dei Filius," in *Decrees of the Ecumenical Councils*, ed. Norman P. Tanner, vol. 2 (Washington, DC: Sheed and Ward, 1990), 804–11.

26. *Sacrosanctum Concilium*, see especially paragraphs 7, 24, 35, 51–52.

liturgical implications for the recognition of the presence of God in the liturgy as a whole.

In addition to their statements about preaching, sacramental celebration, and the fourfold presence of Christ in the liturgical celebration, both *Sacrosanctum Concilium* and *Dei Verbum* also addressed the unified structure of the liturgy itself. This theological move was crucial for the realization of Congar's hope that Catholics would experience "a moment for the Word of God." As long as the Liturgy of the Word could be regarded as separate and inferior to the Liturgy of the Eucharist, the moment for the word of God would remain elusive. In the fall of 1963, *Sacrosanctum Concilium* was promulgated and included the claim that "The two parts which in a sense go to make up the Mass, vis. the liturgy of the word and the eucharistic liturgy, are so closely connected with each other that they form but one single act of worship" (SC 56). In his commentary on *Sacrosanctum Concilium,* Josef Jungmann observed that the intention of this passage was "to thwart the frivolous view of the Sunday obligation, according to which it is sufficient to be present at the sacrificial part of the Mass."[27] The reference to the "single act of worship" expressed the unity of the Liturgy of the Word and the Liturgy of the Eucharist, and thereby elevated the operative understanding of the significance of the Liturgy of the Word. This trajectory, also evident in *Dei Verbum,* would prove to be deeply significant for ecumenical dialogue.

By the time the council came to its conclusion, a stronger image for liturgical unity emerged from the tradition as a bookend to *Sacrosanctum Concilium*'s "two parts" (SC 56). Promulgated at the end of the final session of the council, *Dei Verbum* built on the foundation of *Sacrosanctum Concilium* and referred to the Bread of Life which is offered "to the faithful from the one table of the word of God and the Body of Christ" (DV 21). This image, taken from the biblical christological reference to Jesus as the "Bread of Life" (John 6:35), is also developed in a series of sermons Augustine preached on the Lord's Prayer. In these sermons, Augustine begins by speaking of the daily bread which is "receive[d] from the altar," but quickly makes the connection to "the word of God

27. Josef Andreas Jungmann, "Constitution on the Sacred Liturgy," in *Commentary on the Documents of Vatican II*, ed. Herbert Vorgrimler, vol. 1 (New York: Herder and Herder, 1967), 42.

which is proclaimed every day, that too is bread. [He adds] The fact that it isn't bread for the belly doesn't mean that it isn't bread for the mind."[28] Here the image of bread is applied both to the Eucharist and to the word of God. In *Dei Verbum,* the image of the Bread of Life offered from the "one table" expresses the inherent unity of the word of God and the body of Christ as they are experienced in the liturgy.[29] Even more strongly than *Sacrosanctum Concilium,* it highlights the unity of the single act of worship and the corresponding unity of the single deposit of the word of God (DV 10) as experienced in Scripture and tradition. Echoing Jungmann's point on *Sacrosanctum Concilium,* Joseph Ratzinger points out that despite concerns that the retrieved image of the "one table" would detract from the significance of transubstantiation, those in favor of it argued for it in part because the image was intended to make clear that

> the liturgy of the word was not just a preliminary part of the Mass that could be more or less dispensed with, but of fundamentally equal value with the liturgy that is sacramental in the narrower sense; that the Church, as the community of the body of Christ, is definitely also the community of the Logos, living on the word, so that the "flesh" and

28. Augustine, "Sermon 59," in *Sermons 51-94 (III/3)*, ed. John E. Rotelle, trans. Edmund Hill. The Works of Saint Augustine: A Translation for the 21st Century (New Rochelle, NY: New City Press, 1991), 6.

29. Both Augustine and *Dei Verbum* are clear, however, that the ultimate source of nourishment and revelation is neither word nor sacrament, but Christ the living water. In an earlier homily Augustine develops the eschatological context asking "are we going to go on receiving the eucharist when we have come to Christ himself, and when we have begun to reign with him forever? So the eucharist is our daily bread; but we should receive it in such a way that our minds and not just our bellies find refreshment. . . . But when we finally get there, do you imagine we shall be listening to a book? We shall be seeing the Word itself, listening to the Word itself, eating it, drinking it, as the angels do now. Do the angels need books, or lectures, or readers? Of course not, they read by seeing, since they see the Truth itself, and drink their fill from that fountain, spray which sprinkles us." See Augustine, "Sermon 57," in *Sermons 51-94 (III/3)*, ed. John E. Rotelle, trans. Edmund Hill, The Works of Saint Augustine: A Translation for the 21st Century (New Rochelle, NY: New City Press, 1991), 7. Similar images can be found in the writings of Jerome. See also DV 3.

> "word" in which the "body of Christ," the word made flesh, comes to us becomes our "bread."[30]

The image of the "one table" thus had implications both for the liturgy and for the church's broader understanding of itself. Modifying what Ratzinger referred to as the church's "over-exclusively sacramental way"[31] of understanding itself, the image of the "one table" reoriented the Catholic Church back toward an understanding of itself as nourished not only by the Eucharist but also by the word of God.

The positive effects of this image are clear in the post–Vatican II developments in Catholic liturgical life and theology. Increased attention to the Liturgy of the Word has led to an expanded selection of lectionary texts and a greater emphasis on training for preachers. Catholics of all kinds read the Bible in increasing numbers and self-report that they choose parishes at least in part because of appreciation for the preaching.[32] The image of the "one table," drawn from the traditions of the fourth and fifth centuries, recontextualized in the mid-twentieth-century work of Semmelroth, Rahner, and Schillebeeckx and included in the conciliar documents, provides a foundation from which to build a theology of the word that accounts for sacramentality as well as texts. From this starting point, Catholic theologians have developed diverse theologies of preaching and robust sacramental theologies of language. A deeper appreciation of the ways that symbols function in language has helped theologians to think of sacraments as language events,[33] to consider liturgical and scriptural texts in the context of the church,[34] and to reflect on the symbolic qualities

30. Joseph Ratzinger, "Commentary on *Dei Verbum*," in *Commentary on the Documents of Vatican II*, ed. Herbert Vorgrimler, vol. 3 (New York: Herder and Herder, 1969), 263.

31. Ibid.

32. Mark M. Gray, Mary L. Gautier, and Melissa A. Cidade, "Views from the Pews: Parishioner Evaluations of Parish Life in the United States" (National Association for Lay Ministry; Emerging Models of Pastoral Leadership Project, 2013), 38.

33. See, for example, David N. Power, "Sacrament: Event Eventing," in *A Promise of Presence*, ed. Michael Downey and Richard Fragomeni (Washington, DC: The Pastoral Press, 1992).

34. See, for example, Kevin W. Irwin, *Context and Text: Method in Liturgical Theology* (Collegeville, MN: Liturgical Press, 1994).

of revelation.[35] Catholics across the board have come to understand sacraments not only as rituals but also as events and encounters with God.

As the fiftieth anniversary of *Dei Verbum* approaches, it is clear that while much work has been done, much remains. Mindful of the dualities which can emerge when Scripture and tradition, word and element, Liturgy of the Word and Liturgy of the Eucharist are considered in pairs, this volume will begin with the image from *Dei Verbum* of the "one table of the word of God and Body of Christ"; it will consider the "one table" as a whole from a variety of different perspectives, each of which will highlight the unity of the liturgy. In approaching the complexity of divine revelation offered to Christians in word and sacrament, no one perspective can be entirely adequate. Several starting points from around the table, however, can offer insights which remain hidden when one starts with either word or sacrament as primary.

Chapter 1 of this book begins with a consideration of the lens of biblical prophecy as a means for illuminating the inherent unity of the Liturgy of the Word and the Liturgy of the Eucharist. The prophetic perspective, spanning centuries, biblical books, and liturgical divisions, highlights the similarities between eucharistic symbols and the gestures, words, and actions of the Old Testament prophets. It suggests that in the celebration of the Eucharist, modern Christians can and should see their actions and responsibilities in continuity with the biblical prophets. The links between prophetic and sacramental, Scripture and tradition, ritual practice and everyday life offer a deeper understanding of the proclaimed word and the inherent unity of the liturgical actions spanning time and space.

Building on an understanding of prophetic action driven by the work of the Holy Spirit, the second chapter turns a pneumatological lens on liturgical celebration. Here we will consider the Spirit found in points of difference which can be understood as unifying intersections. Relying on Louis-Marie Chauvet's system of symbolic exchange, which illustrates the role of the Spirit as creator of unity in difference, we will examine liturgical intersections found not only in the space between the Liturgy of the Word and the Liturgy of the Eucharist but also in the points of

35. See, for example, Avery Dulles, "The Symbolic Structure of Revelation," *Theological Studies* 41, no. 1 (March 1980); Avery Dulles, *Models of Revelation* (Maryknoll, NY: Orbis Books, 1992).

difference between liturgical roles and between the ritual celebration and the Christian life. Understood as places of the Spirit, these points of difference become building blocks of unity both for the local community and for the larger church and world.

The third chapter will consider the liturgy through the broad lens of language. Acknowledging the complexity of human language comprised of words, inflections, gestures, and signs, this chapter reflects on the similarities and differences between divine and human language as they have been experienced in Jewish and Christian history. Drawing from the work of Philo and Augustine, as well as from Karl Rahner and other more modern sources, the chapter examines the transformative power of language as it is experienced today in the liturgical context and in what Rahner calls the liturgy of the world.

The fourth chapter provides the broadest lens, considering liturgical unity in light of the sacramentality of all creation. Drawing from sources as diverse as the biblical wisdom tradition, Thomas Aquinas, and the work of Rahner and Chauvet, this chapter suggests that when the liturgy is considered in the graced context of all creation, its inherent unity and raison d'être are revealed. Linking creation, liturgy, and care for the world, the inherent unity of the Liturgy of the Word and Liturgy of the Eucharist can be more clearly appreciated as the source and summit of Christian life when it is seen in a relationship of unity with the Christian life.

As these four perspectives will illuminate, the unity of word and sacrament, Liturgy of the Word and Liturgy of the Eucharist, is best understood when it is approached as *one* table encompassing signs, symbols, words, gestures, actions, encounters, homilies, conversations, meals, and texts. The liturgical metaphor pressed into service to describe revelatory experience expands our understanding of the liturgy as well as of the broader topic of God's revelation offered to humanity in history. When considered together, the four perspectives challenge prior understanding and open the way for a new "moment" of the word of God considered in unifying relationship in the liturgy and in Christian life.

chapter 1

Realizing Unity

The One Table of the Prophetic Word and Body of Christ[1]

In order to better glimpse the unity of word and sacrament, we turn first to a viewpoint that is most frequently associated with the word of God and biblical revelation. The prophetic word of God, which many Catholics encounter primarily in the first reading of the Liturgy of the Word, is often experienced as a blur of strange place names and images, which once heard are soon forgotten. Few homilists undertake to explain or contextualize the odd and sometimes disturbing words and actions of the ancient biblical prophets. By relegating "prophecy" to the exclusive realm of the beginning stages of the Liturgy of the Word, however, we may miss the prophetic words and actions which can be found elsewhere in the liturgy, as well as in the overall Christian call to conversion. When trained on the liturgy as a whole, the lens of biblical prophecy illuminates the unity of action which exists between contemporary celebrations of the Eucharist and the equally radical and symbol-charged actions of the biblical prophets. By considering *Dei Verbum*'s "one table" (DV 21), we will come to see the depths of the whole more clearly.

1. An earlier version of this chapter was published as "Realizing Unity: The One Table of the Prophetic Word and Body of Christ," *Worship* 86, no. 4 (2012): 323–33. Used by permission.

A member of a religious community once commented that prophets are great until you have to live in the same house with one of them. It was not primarily the *words* of the prophet that created cause for concern. Reflection on some of the great prophetic voices of our own time, Martin Luther King, Dorothy Day, Archbishop Oscar Romero, or other prophetic figures in our lives, reveals that the voices of these prophets, while significant, are really only the tip of the iceberg—it is their *actions* which lead to transformative discomfort. Public marches in the face of dogs and fire hoses. The poor and hungry not on the receiving end of a check, but sleeping on the couch, eating at the dining room table, and requesting seconds. People are not considered "prophetic" unless their words are accompanied and supported by actions which are often equally shocking, disconcerting, and ultimately, transformative. In this chapter we will turn first to the work of biblical scholars for insights into the content of the prophetic books often associated with the beginning of the Liturgy of the Word. In the second section, we will examine the symbolic actions of Jesus, particularly those of the Last Supper, through the lens of biblical prophecy. This will lead to a consideration of the prophetic context of eucharistic origins, and by extension, the church itself. The conclusion will consider the liturgical significance, including implications for preaching, of regarding this "one table" through a prophetic lens.

Prophecy as Revelatory of the Presence of God

Biblical scholars point out that while the prophetic books contain many oracles ("the word of the Lord" formula which is often associated with prophecy), they also contain equally significant narrative accounts of prophetic actions. These actions can function symbolically to reveal God's desires and intentions. They can also transform and mediate the human encounter with God through symbols and symbolic actions. The work of Scripture scholars helps to illustrate some of the ways in which the prophetic words and actions described in the Old Testament can be understood as indications and mediations of the transforming presence of God in the centuries before the birth of Christ.

The conventions of liturgical proclamation as well as those of prophetic oracles tend to highlight the verbal and textual elements of the prophetic narratives. In the liturgical context, the lector ascends to the ambo, adjusts the book, and announces: "A reading from the book of the prophet ——." The text is proclaimed from the book, according to the approved translation. The lector concludes with the phrase "The Word of the Lord." The significance of the book and the task of reading are emphasized. Similar conventions found in the narratives themselves have led listeners to focus on the verbal oracles confided by God to the prophets. These oracles are demarcated by what scholars call a "word-event formula."[2] The formula, "the word of the Lord came to me" (e.g., Ezek 6:1), serves to indicate that what follows are to be understood as the words of God proclaimed to the people by means of human language. As Luke Timothy Johnson says, "[t]he human words spoken by the prophet can be called 'God's word' because they communicate to other humans God's perspective on the human situation they share, communicating as well God's vision for a humanity that present circumstances impede."[3] Given this emphasis on the words themselves, it can be too easy to dismiss the dramatic actions as marginal decorations to prophecy, rather than more accurately to regard them as part of the prophetic event itself.

In many cases, however, the words of Scripture also serve to convey the reality of prophetic actions which mediate revelation. In order to examine the dynamic and symbolic qualities of biblical prophecy, we now turn specifically to the topic of prophetic symbols and actions. In addition to the better known prophetic oracles, biblical scholars also speak of prophetic actions or dramas,[4] which can serve as vehicles of revelation. David Stacey offers the following general description of such an event: "When a prophetic drama takes place, an action, a person or persons, and possibly an object belonging to the everyday world are deliberately brought into relationship with some unseen event or reality, usually something on a much larger scale than the drama itself. The dramas point away from themselves toward the unseen element in the conjunction."[5]

2. James Robson, *Word and Spirit in Ezekiel*, ed. Claudia Camp and Andrew Mein, Library of Hebrew Bible/Old Testament Studies (New York: T&T Clark, 2006), 37.

3. Luke Timothy Johnson, *Prophetic Jesus, Prophetic Church: the Challenge of Luke-Acts to Contemporary Christians* (Grand Rapids, MI: Eerdmans, 2011), 44.

4. Stacey prefers the term "drama." See: W. David Stacey, *Prophetic Drama in the Old Testament* (London: Epworth Press, 1990), 21–22.

5. Ibid., 260.

Key to this description are the roles of the ordinary action, person, or object, the relationship of the visible element to the invisible reality, and the universal significance of the event. These characteristics, which are strikingly similar to the characteristics of the sacraments, indicate the presence of prophetic revelation. The results of the divine encounter can vary significantly depending on the circumstances and, presumably, God's intentions. Biblical scholars speak of several different categories of prophetic actions, each of which reveals something about God and which simultaneously effects change in the individual and in the community.

The first category of prophetic action to which we will turn is that of "prophetic actions which point to a divine activity which cannot otherwise be observed."[6] This type of prophetic action reveals God's intentions for humanity, and frequently contains a warning to turn away from sin. Morna Hooker offers the example of the prophet Jeremiah, who smashes pottery in order to indicate God's otherwise unobservable intentions for humanity. Jeremiah is instructed to "Go, buy a potter's earthenware flask. . . . And you shall break the flask . . . and say to them: Thus says the LORD of hosts: Thus will I smash this people and this city, as one smashes a clay pot so that it cannot be repaired" (Jer 19:1, 10-12). Here Jeremiah's action is indicative of God's intentions regarding the destruction of Israel.[7] His words convey part of the message, but it is the symbolic action which underlines and illustrates the message. In this case, the action functions as a warning which urges change through the revelation of God's intentions for Jerusalem. It reveals God's intention, which could not otherwise be known, but does not in itself effect change.

Other categories of prophetic action do more than simply illustrate God's intentions. In some cases the prophet, through his or her actions and experiences, reveals and mediates the salvific presence of God in specific events. Hooker describes these as prophetic actions which "mediate manifestations of divine power in events which bring with them either salvation or judgment."[8] These actions have been understood by the community as God's direct intervention in history through the prophets.

6. Morna Hooker, *The Signs of a Prophet: The Prophetic Actions of Jesus* (Harrisburg, PA: Trinity Press International, 1997), 3.

7. Ibid.

8. Ibid.

One example of this type of prophetic action is the description of Moses' actions at the parting of the Red Sea. Moses' act of stretching out his hand illustrates and makes present the power of the figurative hand of God. Although it is Moses' own physical hand which is stretched out, the text interprets this action as the action of God: "Your right hand, O LORD, magnificent in power, your right hand, O LORD, shattered the enemy" (Exod 15:6). Moses' action is both indicative of God's presence and also brings with it immediate salvation: the Israelites are physically rescued and also recognize God's hidden actions on their behalf.

In still other cases, rather than an intervening action, it is a symbolic vision which conveys the transformative presence of God to humanity. Joseph Blenkinsopp explores the ways in which prophetic symbols operate to convey this transformative presence in the book of Ezekiel. Ezekiel's account of his vision of the valley of bones creates an image for the community:

> A sound started up, as I was prophesying, rattling like thunder. The bones came together, bone joining to bone. As I watched, sinews appeared on them, flesh grew over them, skin covered them on top, but there was no breath in them. Then he said to me: Prophesy to the breath, prophesy, son of man Say to the breath: Thus says the Lord GOD: From the four winds come, O breath, and breathe into these slain that they may come to life. I prophesied as he commanded me, and the breath entered them; they came to life and stood on their feet, a vast army. (Ezek 37:7-10)

In the words of Blenkinsopp, Ezekiel "has provided a powerful visual symbol of the reversal of the life-death process, or the belief in physical resurrection, or the vivifying power of God throughout Jewish and Christian history. . . . The . . . community which has lost its will to survive, is vivified by the spirit activated through the word of God addressed to the community."[9] Here the *image* of the valley of dry bones, offered to Ezekiel in a prophetic vision, acts as a transformative symbol. The image is first manifested visually and aurally to Ezekiel in his prophetic vision. It is then conveyed, by means of descriptive words, to the community.

9. Joseph Blenkinsopp, *A History of Prophecy in Israel*, rev. and enlarged ed. (Louisville: Westminster John Knox, 1996), 178.

This prophetic word-image "vivifies" the community; it transforms them, and has the capacity to do so because it is a manifestation of the power and presence of the Spirit in history.

In the case of Ezekiel's experience, both the symbolic vision and the descriptive words which convey the vision function for the transformation of the community. It can also be the case that the prophet himself or herself is transformed by the prophetic experience and thus becomes a living symbol of God's revelatory presence in the community. This "prophetic way of being in the world," as Johnson puts it, "brings God's will into human history through the words, yes, but also the deeds and character of the prophet."[10] Blenkinsopp offers one example of this in his discussion of the prophet Jeremiah, noting that in the case of Jeremiah, "the person, as much as the spoken word, is the message."[11] Jeremiah's many prophetic actions, the loincloth which he purchased and buried until it rotted (Jer 13:1-11), the earthenware flask which he shattered in the sight of the elders at the Potsherd Gate (Jer 19:1-13), the thongs and yoke-bars which he wore to symbolize servitude to the king of Babylon (Jer 27–28), are not isolated symbolic actions. Together, these actions reflect "the adoption of a certain style of living that dramatizes the rejection of what passes for reality in the society as a whole."[12] Jeremiah's actions point toward a reality that had gone unnoticed by most of the people around him. In the destruction of everyday objects and the wearing of a yoke, Jeremiah's life pointed toward the reality of the deterioration and enslavement of Israel. As Stacey puts it, "the prophet was thought to be so closely in touch with the unseen powers that they were constantly showing themselves through him and to him."[13] This overarching way of life reflects the integration of human personhood as mediator of the divine will. The prophet's very life has become indistinguishable from the prophetic message and is, in the words, actions, and experiences which

10. Johnson, *Prophetic Jesus, Prophetic Church*, 41.

11. Ibid., 146.

12. Ibid., 61.

13. Stacey, *Prophetic Drama*, 67. Elsewhere Stacey states: "The prophet was *himself* a symbol. By his very presence in society, he represented the immanence, the power, and the unpredictability of the divine word" (ibid., 61).

comprise it, itself a transformative symbol of God's revealing and transformative presence in the world.

As a careful look at these examples makes clear, the word of God proclaimed in biblical prophecy is not a disembodied word but an encounter with God which reveals both God's hidden intentions and God's participation in human history. This revelation sometimes comes in the words of prophetic oracles, but it also comes through prophetic actions, symbolic visions, and perhaps most strongly when the prophet him or herself is so united with the will of God that the individual's entire life becomes a prophetic symbol for God's presence in human history.

The Prophetic and Sacramental Life of Jesus

As we have seen, biblical prophecy is not an exclusively verbal undertaking. While prophetic oracles are certainly to be found in Scripture, they are also frequently accompanied by prophetic actions involving symbols. These oracles, actions, and symbols are often found in the life context of an individual whose entire existence has become a symbol of God's revealed presence and intentions. Viewed through the lens of biblical prophecy, Jesus of Nazareth provides an important example of this type of prophet. This section will first consider some actions of Jesus of Nazareth as prophetic according to the categories sketched above. We will then turn specifically to the actions of Jesus within the context of the Last Supper to consider the sacramental origins of Eucharist from the perspective of prophetic action. Finally we will look at the prophetic and sacramental implications for the church.

New Testament scholars point out that the title of prophet was most likely one of the earliest titles applied to the person of Jesus of Nazareth. Citing such actions as Jesus' entry into Jerusalem and the clearing of the temple, Stacey observes that the crowds depicted in the Gospels "would surely have seen him as a new kind of prophetic person at the very least."[14] In the Gospel of Matthew, Peter reports that people think Jesus is Elijah, or Jeremiah, or one of the prophets (Matt 16:14; cf. Mark 6:15; 8:28; Luke 9:8, 19). The crowds may not yet understand fully, but they are certainly

14. W. David Stacey, "The Lord's Supper as Prophetic Drama: The A. S. Peake Memorial Lecture, 1993," *Epworth Review* 21, no. 1 (1994): 68.

acting within reason to think that Jesus is a prophet. Hooker points to the example of the withering of the fig tree in the Gospel of Mark as an example of a prophetic action which indicates God's previously hidden intent to destroy Jerusalem.[15] Johnson observes a trajectory in the Gospel of Luke in which Jesus is recognized as a prophet in the contexts of a healing miracle (Luke 7:16), in a discussion of his identity (Luke 9:8, 19), and finally in the postresurrection account of the journey to Emmaus when the disciples speak of their leader as "a man who was a prophet, mighty in deed and word" (Luke 24:19).[16]

Jesus' own self-understanding also seems to reflect the significance of the prophetic role. In Luke's account of Jesus' rejection at Nazareth, we find Jesus observing that "no prophet is accepted in his own native place" (Luke 4:24). Later in the Gospel of Luke, Jesus predicts his passion in prophetic terms, saying that he must continue on because it is "impossible that a prophet should die outside of Jerusalem" (Luke 13:33).[17] John Meier suggests that throughout his earthly life, "Jesus well understood and often engaged in prophetic-symbolic gestures that proclaimed, and to some degree actualized, the kingdom."[18] Although it is impossible to be certain of Jesus' intentions in performing these gestures, his words and actions are indicative of the lifestyle of an Israelite prophet and of his understanding of himself in similar terms.

From the Christian perspective, the life of Jesus is a clear example of what we have called a prophetic lifestyle in which "the person, as much as the spoken word, is the message."[19] Jesus is more than a prophet, yet, in a comparison with the traits of biblical prophets as they are described in the Old Testament, the life, words, and, actions of Jesus clearly fit the

15. Hooker, *The Signs of a Prophet*, 44. John Meier lists among Jesus' prophetic actions: "his prohibition of fasting coupled with his festive meals with toll collectors and sinners, his exorcisms, his 'triumphal' entry into Jerusalem, his 'cleansing' of the Jerusalem temple, and the symbolic gestures over bread and wine at the Last Supper." John P. Meier, *A Marginal Jew: Rethinking the Historical Jesus*, ed. David Noel Freedman, vol. 3: *Companions and Competitors*, The Anchor Bible Reference Library (New York: Doubleday, 2001), 153.

16. See Johnson, *Prophetic Jesus, Prophetic Church*, 30.

17. See ibid.

18. Meier, *A Marginal Jew*, vol. 3: *Companions and Competitors*, 153.

19. Blenkinsopp, *A History of Prophecy in Israel*, 146.

bill. As Johnson points out, Jesus is not only described as a prophet but also directly compared to the greatest of the Israelite prophets, Moses, and to "the two prophets whose exploits in Scripture are themselves based on Moses, namely Elijah and Elisha."[20] These comparisons serve to indicate that Jesus functions as a particular type of prophet who heals the people like Elijah and Elisha (1 Kgs 17:8-16; 2 Kgs 5:1-14), ascends to God like Elijah (2 Kgs 2:11), is closely linked to the Spirit of God like Elisha (2 Kgs 2:9-12), and, like Moses, both leads the people forward and is associated with powerful forms of divine revelation such as the Ten Commandments given on the mountain (Exod 20:1-21). While the healing miracles occur primarily in the earlier parts of the gospel accounts, Jesus' close association with the Holy Spirit spans the course of his ministry from baptism to ascension. His leadership capacity, present throughout his lifetime, becomes even more important in the final days of his life when he prepares his disciples for the events which will occur.

We now turn specifically to the Last Supper, an event which clearly demonstrates the convergence of prophetic action and Christian sacrament. As noted above, Stacey's characteristics of prophetic drama require that the event involve "an action, a person or persons, and possibly an object belonging to the everyday world [which] are deliberately brought into relationship with some unseen event or reality, usually something on a much larger scale than the drama itself. The dramas point away from themselves towards the unseen element in the conjunction."[21] In the case of the Last Supper, the most significant elements of this prophetic drama are the presence and significance of the Twelve, the actions of the sharing of the bread and cup, and the overarching context of the Passover, which points to the universal implications of the drama.

In the event of the Last Supper, the Twelve play a critical role. On the one hand, they are the close and rather ordinary friends and followers of Jesus gathered for a meal. On the other hand, they also function symbolically, representing humanity both past (the twelve tribes of Israel) and future (the beginning of the church). As Meier puts it, "the mere fact that Jesus the eschatological prophet chose to select twelve Israelite men from among his disciples to form a special group would, in the eyes of his

20. See Johnson, *Prophetic Jesus, Prophetic Church*, 30.

21. Stacey, *Prophetic Drama* 260.

adherents, set in motion the regathering of the twelve tribes, even before these twelve men actually did anything."[22] The fact that the Twelve are already functioning as a prophetic symbol, both passively in their number, and more actively in their work as assistants in the public ministry of Jesus,[23] is important. Their prophetic role can be seen to increase after they undergo prophetic transformation in the Last Supper.

In addition to the symbolic function of the Twelve, Jesus' prophetic actions at the Last Supper also involve the manipulation of the everyday symbols of bread and wine, which function to reveal God's otherwise hidden intentions and to mediate divine power. This is in keeping with the prophetic tradition as described previously. As Hooker points out, both Jeremiah and Jesus interact with "material objects . . . which they 'identified' . . . with something else."[24] In the case of the Last Supper, both the actions of Jesus involving the material objects and the individual material objects themselves are central to understanding the hidden intentions which he seeks to convey.[25] As noted above, for Jeremiah, a potter's work in shaping, reshaping, and even smashing a piece of pottery points to God's hope for and readiness to punish Israel. For Jesus, who also breaks something, the symbolic action functions somewhat differently. As Hooker observes, the symbol of breaking bread differs significantly from the symbol of breaking pottery: "[w]hen you smash a jar into pieces you destroy it, but when you break bread you *share* it."[26] At the Last Supper, the bread, which Jesus identifies with his very self, is broken and shared among the disciples. The sharing of bread points to God's plan that Jesus' body be broken and shared for the good of all. The element itself is central to an adequate interpretation of the prophetic action.

The second element, the cup, which is shared without being broken, is also a part of this complex prophetic drama. In both cases, it is the everyday material element which mediates the action and points beyond itself to a matter of more universal significance. As Stacey observes, prophetic actions sometimes involve "everyday, oft-repeated actions that

22. Meier, *A Marginal Jew*, vol. 3: *Companions and Competitors*, 153.

23. See ibid., 152–63.

24. Hooker, *The Signs of a Prophet*, 48.

25. Ibid.

26. Ibid.

are deliberately taken over and used as prophetic material."[27] Here the breaking and sharing of bread points not to destruction but to the sharing of new life. The cup, which cannot be divided, but is shared by being passed, functions first as a sign of unity. Stacey notes that in the early Pauline account of the institution narrative, Jesus, rather than directly identifying the wine as his blood, says, "this cup is the new covenant in my blood" (1 Cor 11:25; cf. Luke 22:20). In the prior prophetic tradition, Moses sprinkled blood on the people as a sign of their enhanced holiness as part of entry into covenant with God (Exod 24). Building on this past understanding of the covenant,[28] Jesus also points forward to the inbreaking of the kingdom of God, indicating that he will not feast again until "the kingdom of God comes" (Luke 22:18). In the awareness that his life is coming to an end, Jesus takes and shares the cup in a prophetic action which both acknowledges his coming death and conveys that "God will in the end vindicate [God's] cause and . . . prophet by bringing in his kingdom and seating Jesus at the final banquet to drink the festive wine once again."[29] In sharing this cup with Jesus, the disciples are changed; they both take on the obligation of the new covenant in Jesus' blood and signal their hope that they, like Jesus, will share in the eschatological feast, symbolized by the cup. This action can be understood in continuity with the previous experiences shared between Jesus and his disciples. The single cup, passed and shared, thus functions first as a sign of unity and covenantal commitment, while simultaneously pointing forward toward the larger significance of the messianic banquet.

The universal significance of Jesus' actions in the context of the Last Supper is also emphasized by the ritual context of the event. During the celebration of Passover, "Israel looked backwards to the great deliverance of the exodus and forwards to the final deliverance of the messianic age."[30] Stacey adds: "[we] have to interpret the action of Jesus, therefore . . . as dramatizing a work of God that was both past and future, and as

27. Stacey, "The Lord's Supper as Prophetic Drama," 69.

28. Hooker, *The Sign of a Prophet*, 53.

29. John P. Meier, *A Marginal Jew: Rethinking the Historical Jesus*, ed. David Noel Freedman, The Anchor Bible Reference Library, vol. 2: *Mentor, Message, and Miracles* (New York: Doubleday, 1994), 308.

30. Stacey, "The Lord's Supper as Prophetic Drama," 71.

involving the disciples in a task that had partly been completed, but in part lay ahead of them."[31] Here the context of biblical prophecy can assist in parsing the meaning of the symbolic action at the heart of the eucharistic celebration. The meal Jesus shared with his friends functioned in part as a model for Christian sacramental practice. It did so, however, only because it first functioned as a prophetic drama in which the disciples recognized prophetic revelation of universal significance.

In the Last Supper, both a revelatory event and a sacramental model, Jesus seems to look back toward the prophetic tradition and forward toward the needs of the future community. Like other prophets before him, he uses ordinary materials for transformative purposes. The elements of bread and wine are transformed in order to effect transformation in the human beings who engage these elements in the celebration of a ritual meal. From the perspective of biblical prophecy, this transformation may be compared to the transformations effected by Moses' gesture on the shores of the Red Sea. In the prophetic context, Jesus' actions, like those of the prophets before him, mediate the divine action which effects change in salvation history.

Looking forward, the prophetic actions of Jesus indicate the presence of what Hooker calls "the divine activity which was at work, creating and bonding a new community."[32] The innovation here is that through their transformation, this new community has also been empowered to continue the presence and actions of Jesus.[33] They have shared and drunk from the one cup, thus indicating their participation in the new covenant and their hope for the coming of the kingdom of God, which has already begun in the life of Jesus. They have shared and eaten the bread which was identified as the body of Christ and, through the experience of prophetic revelation, have been themselves transformed to take on the identity of the body of Christ.[34] Using similar language, Nathan Mitchell makes the connection to the sacraments: "[S]acramental language does not 'describe' a new community, but *creates* it. . . . While Jesus was at table with his friends the night before he died, the revolutionary 'language of the future' overtook his own paschal language, thereby *presenting*

31. Ibid.
32. Hooker, *The Signs of a Prophet*, 49.
33. Ibid., 50.
34. Ibid., 51.

(not 're-presenting') the meal as something it had never been before—a communion in his body and blood about to be broken for the world's benefit."[35] This transformation for prophetic action, essentially the making of a prophet or the passing on of the prophetic responsibility which would be continued in the sacraments, is unusual in the biblical prophetic tradition. Hooker argues that the only similar example might be that of the transfer of responsibility from Elijah to Elisha in 2 Kings.[36] This transfer, however, was limited to one generation and did not provide for the transfer of prophetic responsibility in perpetuity.

The prophetic actions of Jesus which transform the community of the Twelve thus also provide a mechanism for the continuation of transformative prophetic action in the church (the transformed body of Christ).[37] As Johnson points out, the prophetic context of the Last Supper, understood in continuity with the preaching and actions of both Jesus and the prophets who went before him, makes it clear that the transfer of authority for the future should also be understood in this vein. The leadership bestowed "must be in accord with the prophetic reversal of values expressed in the Sermon on the Plain"[38] and elsewhere in prophetic action and discourse. This transfer of authority, in the form of servant leadership, lays the foundation for understanding the church not only as a sacrament—as indicated by the Second Vatican Council[39]—but also as the place of the continuation of Jesus' prophetic action.

35. Nathan Mitchell, "Sacrament: More Than Meets the Eye," *Worship* 83, no. 4 (2009): 364.

36. Differences include the fact that Elisha requested it, that he had to do something (see Elijah be taken) in order for it to happen, and that the spirit of Elijah did not remain indefinitely, but only for a single generation.

37. See also David N. Power, "A Prophetic Eucharist in a Prophetic Church," in *Eucharist: Toward the Third Millennium* (Chicago: Liturgical Training Publications, 2007), 34.

38. Johnson, *Prophetic Jesus, Prophetic Church*, 107.

39. See for example, *Sacrosanctum Concilium* 10. Retrieving an image found in the works of Augustine, the Second Vatican Council repeatedly referred to the church as a sacrament. The first instance of this is found in the fifth paragraph of the Constitution on the Sacred Liturgy, which describes the origins of the "wondrous sacrament of the whole Church" (SC 5) pouring forth from the side of Jesus crucified on the cross. The image is later found in *Lumen Gentium*, the Dogmatic Constitution on the

The Prophetic and Sacramental Church

Without diminishing the uniqueness of the incarnation of the second person of the Trinity in the person of Jesus of Nazareth, it is clear that Jesus' actions and lifestyle were in continuity with those of the previous prophets of Israel. His actions are indicative of the otherwise hidden intentions of God; they sometimes bring immediate salvation or judgment. They have the capacity to transform those who are affected by them. Jesus is also able to initiate or call future generations of prophets to participate in the perpetuation of his own prophetic hopes and actions through the ritual celebration of the sacraments. This call is indicative of an overarching responsibility to take on the prophetic lifestyle of Jesus in which "the person, as much as the spoken word, is the message."[40] As Johnson points out, the acceptance of this prophetic lifestyle is described very early in the Christian tradition, in the lives of the first Christians depicted in the book of Acts. Just as Jesus can be seen as following in the footsteps of prophetic leaders such as Moses and Elijah and Elisha, so too did the earliest Christians continue to manifest prophetic traits. They are distinctive in their corporate ability to carry on the prophetic tradition of Jesus, particularly in gestures which both reveal and mediate God's presence in history, and in their close association with the Spirit of God. As the centuries progressed, these Christian practices were understood anew in the forms of sacraments that ritualized the prophetic actions of Jesus.

Among the practices of the early Christian community that can be seen as continuations of the work of Jesus (and of the prior prophets) are their healing miracles, which echo those of Jesus, Elijah, and Elisha, as well as their practice of sharing all things in common, which seems to be a deliberate allusion to the vision of God described in the book of Deuteronomy. Jesus' many acts of healing are clearly attested in the New Testament. These actions, which, like Moses' action to part the Red Sea, both indicate and effect salvation, are a part of the prophetic legacy which is carried on in the book of Acts. The many healings in Acts, from Peter's action to heal

---

Church, which refers to the church as the sacrament of God's saving unity (LG 9). This description carries with it the connotations of transformation and signification which are associated with the seven ritual sacraments.

40. Blenkinsopp, *A History of Prophecy in Israel*, 146.

the lame man in Acts 3 to his raising the widow Tabitha (Acts 9:36-42), to Paul's healings and exorcisms later in Acts, all echo Jesus' actions and the actions of prophetic leaders such as Elijah, who restored the widow's son to life (1 Kgs 17:17-24), and Elisha, who saved another widow and her sons from slavery and debt (2 Kgs 4). In all of these cases, and in the case of Moses' gesture to part the Red Sea (Exod 15:6), God's presence is both signified and effected. God's intentions for the sick, poor, and widowed are made clear, and those who are the objects of the prophet's actions experience salvation from their immediate difficulties and function as both the signs and the effects of God's intentions in the world.

In yet another instance of a symbolic action that both reveals and mediates God's presence in history, the book of Acts describes the earliest Christians as dedicated to sharing all things in common and giving freely to those who were in need (Acts 2:45). As Johnson points out, this action alludes to a passage in the Book of Deuteronomy which describes the vision of God in which "since the LORD, your God, will bless you abundantly in the land the LORD, your God, will give you to possess as a heritage, there shall be no one of you in need" (Deut 15:4).[41] In the visual and literary embodiment of this vision in the community life of the church, the earliest Christians both reveal God's otherwise unseen intentions for humanity and mediate the presence of God to those who would otherwise have lacked basic necessities. As a community, they act in a manner which is consistent with the symbolic revelations of the Old Testament prophets as well as with the preaching and prophetic manner of life displayed by Jesus.

As was the case with prophets before them, the prophetic actions of these early Christians are both initiated and sustained by the Spirit of God. Just as Elisha received a "double portion" of the Spirit (2 Kgs 2:9-11), and Jesus received the Spirit in his baptism in the Jordan, so the church receives the Spirit at Pentecost. As Johnson points out, the prophetic trajectory is clear from the disciples' own experience of the Spirit of God that enables them to speak in different languages (Acts 2:4), to Peter's preaching on a passage in which the prophet Joel speaks of a time when God will "pour out a portion of [God's] Spirit on all flesh" (Acts 2:17), to the mention of the prophetic "signs and wonders" (Acts 2:22) performed

41. See Johnson, *Prophetic Jesus, Prophetic Church*, 111–13.

by Jesus.[42] Peter's interpretation of these experiences can be seen to establish the church's position in Israel's prophetic history. The prophetic tradition continued to evolve in early Christianity in the establishment of ritual baptism as an experience of what Hooker calls "divine activity . . . at work creating and bonding a new community."[43] This becomes clear when those present respond to Peter's invitation to "Repent and be baptized, every one of you, in the name of Jesus Christ for the forgiveness of your sins; and you will receive the gift of the holy Spirit" (Acts 2:38), and as the early communities continued the ritual celebration of the Last Supper. In these ritual practices, the early church continued the manipulation of everyday symbols that functioned both to reveal God's otherwise unseen intentions and to mediate divine power.[44] These actions, as was the case at the Last Supper, function in the context of the church to "create and bond a new community."[45] The sacramental evolution of these ideas becomes clear in the fifth-century preaching of Augustine, who famously told his *infantes*, "You are beginning to receive what you have also begun to be."[46] He was referring of course to the body of Christ, which, as we have seen, is the risen body of a prophet. If the origins of the Eucharist lie in the realm of prophetic drama and the transfer of prophetic responsibility, then Christians, at least by the time of Augustine, recognized themselves as called to prophetic transformation as often as they participate in the liturgy.

As was the case with the prophets before them, this transformation is never for personal fulfillment, but rather for God's purposes in the world. As Stacey puts it, "we must believe that our Lord was not simply enabling Peter and Andrew and James and John to get themselves sorted out in the upper room."[47] The perspective of prophetic action demands that those who celebrate the Christian sacraments see themselves as heirs

42. Ibid., 62.

43. Hooker, *The Signs of a Prophet*, 49.

44. Hooker, *The Signs of a Prophet*, 3.

45. Ibid., 49.

46. Augustine, "Sermon 228B," in *Sermons on the Liturgical Seasons*, ed. John E. Rotelle, The Works of Saint Augustine: A Translation for the 21st Century (New Rochelle, NY: New City Press, 1993), 4.

47. Stacey, "The Lord's Supper as Prophetic Drama," 73.

responsible for the continuation of the prophetic lifestyle of Jesus lived in the Holy Spirit.[48] This of course has ethical implications beyond the strictly liturgical setting—as can be seen in the lives of people like Oscar Romero and Dorothy Day who have integrated word and symbolic action to live the call to Christian prophetic lifestyle.

Conclusion: The Table of Prophetic Action

For most Catholics, encounter with biblical prophecy comes primarily in the modern-day liturgical context of the first reading. Removed from their original cultural and textual contexts, however, these short passages are often mystifying, and certainly quite foreign to the cultural context of the twenty-first century. It is rarely immediately clear that they are part of the same table as the body of Christ. Nonetheless, the lens of prophetic action, broadly understood, can offer a helpful perspective on twenty-first-century liturgical celebration. It can lead to a deeper understanding of the word of God, the sacraments, and the unified "table of the word of God and the Body of Christ" (DV 21), from which the Bread of Life is offered to the faithful.

As Thomas Aquinas points out in his discussion of the sacraments in the Third Part of the *Summa Theologiae*, God allows human beings "to achieve an awareness of things which they do not know through things which they do know."[49] The earliest followers of Jesus had no knowledge of the doctrine of the incarnation of the Second Person of the Trinity. The salvific and transformative actions of God in the prophets, however, were well known to them. They likewise knew from their tradition that all prophecy is a result of divine action and human bodily mediation. Recognizing Jesus as a prophet, they began to understand him, and perhaps eventually themselves, as part of the body of Christ. In the

48. David Power argues that "[h]eard at a sacramental celebration, the prophecies invite a remembrance of the counterstories . . . from this there may spring a lamentation, which calls for an entering into the Christ story and the Christ event within a new horizon of conversion." David N. Power, *Sacrament: The Language of God's Giving* (New York: Crossroad 1999), 364.

49. Thomas Aquinas, *Summa Theologiae* (New York: Blackfriars and McGraw-Hill, 1963), III, q. 60, a. 2.

modern-day liturgical context, it may be argued that believers have the opposite experience. Far removed from biblical prophecy, modern believers understand—at least in general terms—that Jesus is God Incarnate and is present to them in the eucharistic celebration. This, however, does not help to explain the first reading on the Fourth Tuesday of Lent, in Year A, in which Ezekiel's process of wading through water of varying depths is described in great detail (Ezek 47:1-9; 12). When the modern believer begins with an understanding of Jesus' actions as prophetic, it can make it possible to relate to the prophets who went before him. This perspective can in turn highlight the significance of the divine will at work in other prophets, thus offering the possibility for liturgical continuity between the familiar actions of Jesus and the less familiar, and sometimes bewilderingly foreign, actions of his prophetic predecessors.

The lens of biblical prophecy can also help modern-day Christians to recognize that prophecy is not exclusively the "word" of God any more than sacraments are exclusively the "symbols" which effect transformation. Both prophecy and sacrament rely on words, symbols, and actions for the purposes of facilitating the divine-human encounter in history. An understanding of prophecy emphasizes the enduring importance of the human body and human experience for the mediation of divine revelation in salvation history. The creative, transforming word of God is rarely a disembodied word. This is most clearly seen in the incarnation, but it also is seen in the words, symbols, and actions of the biblical prophets, in the preaching of Jesus and the disciples, and in the sacramental celebrations of Christians today. It is not possible to relegate "word" to one end of the liturgical table and "symbol" to the other. Word and symbol combined in both prophetic and sacramental actions are the building blocks of biblical prophecy and of Christian sacramental celebration. The liturgical proclamation of biblical prophecy thus has the potential to function as a stark reminder of the mediation of the word of God in human language, symbols, and experience.

Finally, the prophetic perspective deals directly with an understanding of the inherent unity of the "bread of life [which is] offere[d] to the faithful from the one table of the word of God and the Body of Christ" (DV 21). While Christians do not always think of themselves as prophetic, one can argue that as a church, they are called to both prophetic and to sacramental witness in the world. The actions of which they are capable can and should reveal and mediate God's presence in the world. This capacity and vocation is grounded in the ritual experiences of the sacraments. In the ritual expression of Jesus' prophetic actions, particularly in baptism and Eucharist, Christians both reveal and mediate the presence of God and are bonded into a new community, called to prophetic witness and action in the world. In this context the prophetic elements of the Liturgy of the Word can be understood as a transformative model of the life which the Liturgy of the Eucharist makes possible in history. Far from separate entities, the liturgical experience as a whole has the capacity to nurture the faithful for prophetic witness through the Spirit of God present in word and sacrament.

chapter 2

"And [Also] with Your Spirit?"

Finding the Spirit of Unity in the Liturgical Celebration

The recent translation of the third edition of the Roman Missal brought with it a renewed awareness of the complexity of liturgical unity. Debates over translation guidelines, ecumenical implications, elevated language, and comprehensibility were heard in classrooms, pews, and church basements around the English-speaking world. One of the initial challenges presented by this new translation was the assembly's frequently repeated response to the presider's greeting. In the wake of the familiar "and also with you," the newly translated phrase "and with your spirit" signaled to some English-hearing ears a dualistic view of the human person as body on the one hand and spirit on the other. In the months following the adoption of the new translation, the response "and *also* with your Spirit," found in neither the Sacramentary nor in the Roman Missal became, in many parishes, the de facto response to the presider's greeting. While this phrase clearly reflected a transitional phase between one set of ritual words and another, it also highlighted a curious tension between the "old" response, which might now be heard as having been directed at the whole person of the presider, and the newly translated response, which could indicate the more narrowly construed "spirit" of the presider.

In the popular usage of most English speakers, "spirit" is that which is not body. It can refer to the "animating or vital principle . . . that which gives life to the physical organism, in contrast to its purely material elements,"[1] or to an "incorporeal or immaterial being, as opposed to *body* or *matter*; being or intelligence conceived as distinct from, or independent of, anything physical or material."[2] Both definitions present "spirit" in contrast to that which is physical or embodied, thus suggesting to the hearer that the greeting is offered exclusively to the priest's invisible spirit or soul rather than to his whole being.[3] Such dualism is underscored by some other newly translated phrases, such as the response, after the *Agnus Dei*, which reads "but only say the word and my *soul* shall be healed"[4] [italics mine]. While body/spirit dualism does not seem to be the intention of the translation,[5] the variety of technical theological meanings

1. *Oxford English Dictionary*, 2nd ed., s.v. "spirit."

2. Ibid.

3. Dominic Serra agrees, noting that "[i]n catechesis, it will be important to point out that the greeting to the priest's 'spirit' does not establish a kind of dualism that may suggest that the spirit rather than the body is honored by the greeting. Spirit here has the very opposite sense as the fullness of humanity." Dominic E. Serra, "The Introductory Rite: Theology of the Latin Text and Rite," in *A Commentary on the Order of Mass of the Roman Missal: A New English Translation*, ed. Edward Foley, et al. (Collegeville, MN: Liturgical Press, 2011), 129.

4. See the 2010 ICEL translation of *Missale Romanum* 2002; Foley, et al., eds., *A Commentary on the Order of Mass of the Roman Missal: A New English Translation* (Collegeville, MN: Liturgical Press, 2011).

5. A FAQ available on the USCCB website in the months surrounding the adoption of the new translation explained the phrase as follows: "[t]he expression *et cum spiritu tuo* is only addressed to an ordained minister. Some scholars have suggested that *spiritu* refers to the gift of the spirit he received at ordination. In their response, the people assure the priest of the same divine assistance of God's spirit and, more specifically, help for the priest to use the charismatic gifts given to him in ordination and in so doing to fulfill his prophetic function in the Church." United States Conference of Catholic Bishops, "Welcoming the Roman Missal Third Edition: Frequently Asked Questions," http://www.usccb.org/prayer-and-worship/the-mass/frequently-asked-questions/notes-on-the-new-translation-of-the-missale-romanum.cfm. Accessed July 9, 2014. Anscar Chupungco rejects this interpretation, stating that "[t]he interpretation that wishes to associate the Holy Spirit or the spirit of the priesthood with this liturgical formula has no solid theological or liturgical basis." Chupungco instead suggests "a comprehensive catechesis grounded on a theological anthropology that finds resonance in the *Magnificat*." Anscar J. Chupungco, "The Introductory Rites: The ICEL 2010 Translation," in Foley, *A Commentary on the Order of Mass of the Roman Missal*, 138.

and connotations of "spirit" (or *pneuma* or *ruah*) are perhaps not the first that come to mind when one offers the greeting on a Sunday morning.[6] A dualistic understanding of these phrases does not reflect the depths of the Catholic tradition on human personhood, but does recall a lingering dualism which, although undercutting the sacramental tradition, remains strong in some strands of Christian theology.

Despite the dictionary definitions, a renewed awareness of the liturgical role of the *Holy* Spirit—should this be a result of the adoption of the new translation—far from encouraging dualism, in fact highlights the inherent unity of the liturgy, and indeed the relationship between matter and spirit on which the sacramental system rests. Recent developments in sacramental theology have given greater attention to the pneumatological implications of sacramental celebration. This work points to the inherent unity of body and spirit, priest and assembly, liturgical elements and Christian life. In this chapter, we will first consider a theological framework which seeks to avoid the problems of hierarchical dualism by replacing the metaphysical framework with one grounded in human life experience as understood by the social sciences. This system, adapted by sacramental theologian Louis-Marie Chauvet, directs attention to a "third term," which is to be found in the relationships between human subjects. When this "third term" is considered in the relationship between God and humanity, it turns our attention away from ourselves as human subjects and directs us toward consideration of the Holy Spirit who, Chauvet suggests, is to be found in the differences which exist in relationships. Having considered Chauvet's trinitarian approach, we will then turn to three key moments in the liturgy in which the work of the Holy Spirit can be detected. These moments of difference occur throughout the liturgy and illuminate the inherent unity that can, with the help of the Spirit, emerge out of difference. Grounded in a theological understanding of the Spirit of God received by all believers at their baptisms, the unity of the "one table" is seen not only in the relationship between the Liturgy of

6. As Peter Jeffery notes, "many people, both laity and priests, will miss all these allusions. And where texts or practices are no longer understood, odd and misleading explanations, including some non-Biblical concepts of 'spirit,' will rise almost spontaneously to fill the vacuum." Peter Jeffery, *Translating Tradition: A Chant Historian Reads* Liturgiam Authenticam (Collegeville, MN: Liturgical Press, 2005), 94.

the Word and the Liturgy of the Eucharist but also in points of difference throughout the celebration as a whole.

Embodied Relationships and the System of Symbolic Exchange

The challenges of dualism are not new developments in the Christian tradition. The temptation to value excessively the spiritual to the detriment of the physical has plagued Christians since early Gnostic writings dating to the second century. In the twentieth century, postmodern sacramental theologians have addressed this tendency with proposals for sacramental frameworks which rely on systems other than metaphysics.[7] Arguing that the metaphysical system has inclined Christianity toward a worldview which contrasts material and spiritual elements of reality,[8] theologian Louis-Marie Chauvet offers a sacramental framework structured around the anthropological system of symbolic exchange. This system, which relies on an understanding of the symbolic order borrowed from Heidegger and the social sciences, offers a triadic rather than dyadic structure, and thus simultaneously opens the doors for a more trinitarian and less dualistic theological approach. In so doing, it provides a helpful framework for recognizing liturgical unity through the lens of pneumatology.

Chauvet defines the symbolic order as that which designates the "meaningful organization of the many elements that compose a properly human existence. It precedes every single person since it is within it that one becomes a 'subject' (or a 'person')."[9] In his use of the symbolic order, Chauvet decentralizes both the individual subject and the spiritual element of humanity. This is not to say that he disregards subjects or spirits, but rather

7. For a clear and helpful overview of the postmodern critique of metaphysics, see Nathan Mitchell, "Mystery and Manners: Eucharist in Post-Modern Theology," *Worship* 79, no. 2 (2005): 135–40. See also John H. McKenna, "Eucharistic Presence: An Invitation to Dialogue," *Theological Studies* 60, no. 2 (1999).

8. This argument can be found in Louis-Marie Chauvet, *Symbol and Sacrament: A Sacramental Reinterpretation of Christian Existence*, trans. Patrick Madigan and Madeleine Beaumont (Collegeville, MN: Liturgical Press, 1995), chaps. 1–4.

9. See Chauvet, *The Sacraments: The Word of God at the Mercy of the Body* (Collegeville, MN: Liturgical Press, 2001), 2.

that he recontextualizes them in a greater whole.[10] In so doing, he seeks to present human language and human bodies not as obstacles to relationship with God, as they have sometimes been regarded, but rather as aspects of the self which mediate relationship. It thus becomes possible to consider material realities, which Chauvet suggests metaphysics has tended to dismiss as obstacles, as instead "the milieu within which human beings learn, at their expense, to accede to their own truth, and by the same token, accept to hear the call of truth, which is greater than themselves."[11] Human language and embodiment are thus understood not as the enemy of the spiritual, but as the necessary milieu for spiritual experience.

Within this context, individual human beings do not take center stage, but are understood, and come to understand themselves, within a particular cultural context. Individual humans, or "I-bodies"[12] as Chauvet calls them, are "structured by the system of values or symbolic network of the group to which each person belongs."[13] Human beings derive meaning and identity from these networks, which can include the church. Since these cultural and linguistic contexts preexist any individual, the individual must make sense of herself and her world both in relationship with others and in a culture she has not created. All relationships, both among human beings and between human beings and God, play out against the backdrop which is already given.

As the individual finds her place in culture and in relationships, she does so not as a disembodied spirit but as an "I-body." An "I-body" is not

10. Chauvet is critical of what he calls a "visceral *anthropocentrism*" (Chauvet, *Symbol and Sacrament*, 28). Because metaphysics starts with the certitude of the self, Chauvet suggests that it encourages human beings to measure everything else that they encounter against the self that they know themselves to possess. This leads to a subject-object dichotomy with regards to one's surroundings and also to God. Chauvet points to theology's tendency to assign value to grace (indulgences, penances, etc.) as another problematic aspect of this issue.

11. Ibid., 6.

12. As Chauvet describes it, an individual, or "I-body[,] exists only as woven, inhabited, spoken by [the] *triple body* of culture, tradition and nature." Chauvet, *Symbol and Sacrament*, 150.

13. Kevin W. Irwin, "The *petit* Chauvet on the Sacraments," *Antiphon* 6, no. 3 (2001): 51–52. In other words, this radically inclusive understanding of body implies a sense of sacramentality which supports Chauvet's entire project.

simply the outside shell of the human being, but is the person herself, who encounters the world as "the primordial place of every symbolic joining of the 'inside' and the 'outside.' "[14] The "I-body" is the point of contact for all relationships, the place of joining between the individual and the other. As Chauvet puts it, it is only as bodies that humans exist "in the world in a very particular way . . . the body is the human 'way' of inhabiting the otherness of the world as a home, a familiar dwelling."[15] Far from being an obstacle to be overcome, this place of differentiated connection is the place in which relationships are realized.

For Christians, for whom the "I-body" is also the place of joining between God and the individual in the sacraments, the experience of the Holy Spirit offered in baptism both shapes them into what Chauvet calls the liturgical "we" responding to God in the liturgy and the prophetic body of Christ called to participative cocreation of the world. The Spirit is found at points of intersection in relationships in which individuals come to understand both their own distinctive identity and simultaneously their own corporate place in shared culture. The "I-body" is required for these experiences. It is only through our bodies that humans are able to interact with others as individuals and as members of a society. These embodied relationships are mediated by exchanges which take place in the material world and in language. Exchanges, of what Chauvet calls "gifts," are the symbolic economy which allows multifaceted relationships to function. These gifts, which may be as small as a smile offered as return for a verbal greeting, are given freely back and forth, within a cultural milieu which dictates that any gift received obligates the receiver to offer a return gift. In this exchange, Chauvet observes, "[t]he true objects being exchanged are the subjects themselves."[16] The material value of any symbolic objects exchanged is thus inconsequential.

14. Chauvet, *Symbol and Sacrament*, 147.

15. Ibid.

16. Ibid., 106. Chauvet demonstrates this with his example of purchasing Girl Scout cookies. He observes: "If the few dollars I give to buy . . . cookies from the Girl Scouts is 'symbolic,' it is not because it is such a paltry sum, but because this purchase constitutes for me *an effective mediation to renew my connections* with these organizations in which I wish to have a stake without being a member or active participant and because this effectiveness is not essentially a function of the size of

This system of symbolic exchange functions both on the human-human level and the human-divine level. On the human level, symbolic exchange may manifest itself in words, actions, or the symbolic exchange of goods. The liturgical greeting, for instance, can be understood in this context. The greeting "The Lord be with you" requires some sort of response or acknowledgment. Failure to respond to a greeting indicates rudeness, or the breakdown of a relationship that is built on the exchange of words and symbols. It is only through the body that words and symbols can be offered, received, and interpreted, and that human beings can situate themselves, in response to one another, in their cultural contexts. The human return gift of gratitude (or acknowledgment) takes its meaning from the cultural milieu and is "veri-fied" by a return gift of words or gestures which can be perceived by the senses. This process of exchange applies both to interactions between humans and between God and humanity. As we will see below, the Holy Spirit is present at each of these points of intersection.

In the context of the divine-human relationship, God is the primary gift-giver, who freely offers a graced world to humanity.[17] In order to maintain the relationship, human beings offer a return gift. As finite beings, they can never give a return gift equal in value to the gifts that God gives, but they can offer recognition and gratitude through symbolic exchange. Chauvet emphasizes that, as in human relationships, a comparison of the material value of the gifts is never helpful. Even as no material value can be attached to the liturgical greeting, neither can value be assigned to God's gift of grace.[18] Only a *symbolic* expression of gratitude is expected, and indeed, required, for the health of the relationship. By "symbolic expression" Chauvet means an expression which is both a mediation of something beyond itself and yet something which "touches *the most real* part of our identity."[19] The symbol of gratitude is

---

my contribution." The symbol of the Girl Scout cookie purchase becomes *more real* because it mediates experience and intent. Chauvet, *Symbol and Sacrament*, 129.

17. Chauvet makes his case for this in ibid., 99–120.

18. "Grace can in no way be considered an object or a value" (ibid., 7). Alternatively, Chauvet suggests that we think of "*Grace as a question, grace as a non-thing, grace as a non-value*" (ibid., 45).

19. Ibid., 130.

most prominently offered in the eucharistic liturgy and is then verified by actions of ethical practice.

Chauvet's critique of the metaphysical system and introduction of the system of symbolic exchange as theological framework leads him to attend not to the opposition of body and spirit, but instead to the points of intersection between human beings who encounter others by means of their whole selves. He sees the body as "the *binding*, the space in the middle where both identity and difference are symbolically connected under the authority of the Other."[20] In the process of relating to the other, humans build up their individual and cultural identities, realizing themselves and their world in what Chauvet calls "the space in the middle."[21] In this relational context, bodies are not barriers to relationship, but function instead as the necessary means for navigating the system of symbolic exchange. In their navigation of the system of symbolic exchange, individuals are constantly shaped by the system and in turn participate in God's creative work through their own contributions to the world.

In the specific context of Christianity, Chauvet examines the *differences* between individual human beings and between human beings and God according to a similar approach. It is in these points of difference between human beings that "the Spirit sets up communication between them. By opening up a *lack* between them, it enables them not to fail to meet one another."[22] As we will see below, in Chauvet's system, these *differences* which could be perceived as tensions between polarities, as well as the *differences* between God and humanity, are in fact the points of intersection in which the work of the Spirit can be found. It is in the initial absence, or lack of connection, that the Spirit creates unity.

Just as contemporary worshippers may be challenged to understand themselves as recipients of the prophetic tradition, so do they also recognize a distinction between their own experiences of the sacraments in the twenty-first century and the inaugural words and actions attributed to Jesus, which ground our present-day sacramental rituals. The believer mourns the loss (to history) of the unmediated presence of

20. Ibid., 147.

21. Ibid.

22. Ibid., 522. Chauvet goes on to add that "just as in opening in each person the absence of God, it enables them not to fail to meet God."

Jesus. In the very acceptance of loss, however, the person finds herself moving toward relationship with God. "[I]n opening in each person the absence of God, [the Spirit] enables them not to fail to meet God."[23] Emphasizing the pneumatological perspective, Chauvet warns against an excessively incarnational approach in which the sacraments are seen as "the somehow static prolongations of the incarnation."[24] Such an approach diminishes the sacraments through dualistic comparison to the past, physical, body of Christ, leading the believer to focus on something which is both immaterial and unattainable. It is in this desire for something that cannot be, in the acknowledgment of loss, that we find the place of the Holy Spirit.[25]

This pneumatological approach to sacramental theology is grounded in the paschal mystery, broadly defined as stretching from incarnation to Parousia.[26] It offers a starting point which, by highlighting the role of the Spirit in the space between *difference*, can help to avoid the dualisms of then and now, physical and spiritual, "real" and symbolic, which can in turn undercut the sacramental significance of liturgical celebrations. To understand the liturgy as a whole, as a "living memorial"[27] which, while rooted in the past, also affects the present and indeed the future, attention to God's continuous action in history is required. This action throughout history and pointing into the future is driven by the Spirit, "the personal name traditionally given to what, *of God*, gives present and future vigor to such a memorial of the past."[28] With an eye to the work

23. Ibid.

24. Chauvet, *The Sacraments*, 160.

25. "The Spirit is thus at the place of our desire. It is the *Openness* in God's very self, the Openness that is constitutive of God's very self, an Openness it inscribes between persons and within each person. Difference between God and God, establishing their communion (theology), difference between God and humans, establishing their possible communication (economy), the Spirit is this Difference of God taking body (anthropology) in the difference between human subjects—from which springs all reciprocity—and at the same time, within each subject, the difference between body and word—in that place where the body itself may come forth as true word." Chauvet, *Symbol and Sacrament*, 522–23. See also ibid., 528.

26. Ibid., 159–60.

27. Ibid., 510.

28. Ibid., 511.

of the Holy Spirit in history, it becomes clear that God's presence is *both* then and now, both physical and spiritual, both real and symbolic, both present and absent.[29] The presence of the Spirit in past, present, and future points to the impossibility of claiming the liturgy for any particular time and place. It points to Christ's presence and absence at any given point in history, offering transformation to believers, yet resisting ownership.

Even as Christians may struggle with acceptance of the loss of the physical presence of Jesus in history, they also struggle with the loss inherent in the central mystery of Christianity—the cross. Here, where immortal divinity is held in tension with broken humanity and where the visceral *absence* of God is most keenly felt, is also a radical point of difference and loss. It is here, however, in the "*Openness* in God's very self, the Openness that is constitutive of God's very self, an Openness it inscribes between persons and within each person,"[30] that the Holy Spirit is found in the immanent Trinity. This Openness within God, most evident on the cross, is not a *difference* of "distance and separation,"[31] but rather one of unified otherness. As Chauvet reminds us, "Otherness is the symbolic place where all communication can take place."[32] This is the point of "[d]ifference between God and God, establishing their communion (theology)"[33] according to the system of symbolic exchange in which the humanity and divinity of the Second Person of the Trinity, the *difference* between Father and Son, requires what Chauvet calls

29. Without the work of the Holy Spirit, "the memorial would either refer to an ahistorical and mythic Christ or to a Jesus viewed as a mere prophet or an exemplary martyr. In neither case would it be any longer a *sacramental* memory, that is, one implying the involvement of the Risen Crucified in the historical 'today' of believers. In order for the past of what is commemorated in the narrative of the institution . . . to be sacramentally given us in the present and to open a future for us, the Spirit must bring it to the memory of the Church." Ibid., 510.

30. Ibid., 522–23, 528.

31. Ibid., 503.

32. Ibid.

33. "The Spirit is thus at the place of our desire. It is the *Openness* in God's very self, the Openness that is constitutive of God's very self, an Openness it inscribes between persons and within each person." Chauvet, *Symbol and Sacrament*, 522–23. See also ibid., 528.

"a *third term*."[34] This third term is "Spirit," the otherness which, in the system of symbolic exchange, facilitates unitive communication rather than distance. The Holy Spirit, functioning as a third term within the immanent Trinity, also plays a similar role in the relationship between humanity and God as experienced in the economic Trinity. Drawing on the christological work of Walter Kasper and Jürgen Moltmann,[35] Chauvet suggests that in the divinity which is crossed out, "*God reveals God in what is most different from God.* God reveals the divine self ultimately as God when God 'crosses out' God in humanity."[36] The point of difference here is the place of God's revelatory self-communication. The role of the Holy Spirit in the difference between humanity and divinity is what makes "communication (economy)"[37] possible, opening the doors to the process of symbolic exchange by which human beings find it possible to relate to God. Just as human relationships are built on the exchange of gifts and gratitude, this *difference* between God and humanity allows humanity to respond to God's gift of self-revelation and offer its own gratitude (Eucharist) and corporality (ethical practice) as the body of God in history.[38] Thus, the *difference* leads, perhaps surprisingly, to unity between God who remains physically absent and human beings who are transformed to be the body of Christ in the world. As Chauvet puts it, "[t]he paradox of the Spirit is this: it makes one participate in God in the same measure as it maintains God's radical difference."[39] It is the Spirit, who "write[s] the very difference of God in the body of humanity,"[40] making it possible for them to participate in God's will for creation.

In shifting perspectives, both on the relationships between human beings and on the relationship between God and humanity, it becomes

34. Ibid., 510.

35. Chauvet refers specifically to Walter Kasper, *Jesus the Christ* (Mahwah, NJ: Paulist Press, 1976), and to Jürgen Moltmann, *The Crucified God: The Cross of Christ as the Foundation and Criticism of Christian Theology* (Minneapolis, MN: Fortress Press, 1993).

36. Chauvet, *The Sacraments*, 163. See also Chauvet, *Symbol and Sacrament*, 492–509.

37. Chauvet, *Symbol and Sacrament*, 522–23. See also ibid., 528.

38. Ibid., 509–11.

39. Ibid.

40. Chauvet, *The Sacraments*, 166.

possible to envision a sacramental system that understands relationships not as binary but as conducted in the context of a "third term." Anthropologically, this third term can be understood as the cultural context that precedes every human being and that supports each person as she comes into her own subjectivity. Theologically, the third term can be understood as the Holy Spirit, who is the point of difference and unity in relationship. When applied to the liturgical context, the pneumatological perspective lays the groundwork for a liturgical celebration which simultaneously finds God in the midst of difference and which enables the transformation of Christians who become the body of Christ in the world. We now turn to three liturgical moments in which attention to the role of the Holy Spirit, understood as the point of unity within difference, can help us not only to appreciate each liturgical action more deeply but also to see it as a moment which illustrates the strength of the unity of the one table.

"That . . . We May Be Gathered into One by the Holy Spirit"[41]

Gathered around the "one table of the word of God and Body of Christ" (DV 21), instances of unity and difference abound. It is no easy process to allow oneself to be formed by the Holy Spirit into the corporate body of Christ. To attend to the role of the Holy Spirit in the eucharistic liturgy, we will examine three liturgical moments which invite deeper reflection on unity and difference. The first is the homiletic moment when the preacher addresses the assembly both as one with them in prayer and as one who is charged to speak a word of grace. The second is the moment of the epiclesis, when the community prays that the Spirit might be sent upon the gifts of bread and wine. This moment marks the difference between that which is and that which is becoming. The third moment is the moment of separation—"Go forth, the Mass is ended."[42] This moment marks the unity in difference between pew and parking lot.

In liturgical preaching, several instances of difference become obvious. The first is the movement into the role of preacher. Whether it is

41. "Eucharistic Prayer II," in Foley, et al., *A Commentary on the Order of Mass of the Roman Missal*, 307.

42. "The Concluding Rites," in Foley, et al., *A Commentary on the Order of Mass of the Roman Missal*, 625.

the presider who has thus far provided ritual leadership or a member of the assembly who has thus far participated from the pews, a similar role change occurs. The difference between assembly and preacher solidifies when the preacher turns to the assembly, addresses them in the first person, and opens up what Chauvet considers to be the space necessary for relationship. If there were no difference between preacher and assembly, there could be no communicative exchange, and thus no relationship. The difference sets up the space for the necessary unity of the shared event, the homily, whose Greek root, *homilein,* means table conversation. When the preacher begins to speak, a second difference may sometimes manifest itself. While Christians profess the belief that the Holy Spirit guides the church's preaching, in practice, the preaching is sometimes experienced as somewhat less than divine. The preacher may be inept, or the assembly may be out of sorts. The difference between preacher and assembly may seem overwhelming and lacking the relational unity of Chauvet's ideal. A pneumatological lens on the liturgical celebration can help to illuminate the unity to be found in these points of difference. In both cases, the Holy Spirit may be glimpsed in the points of relational intersection between preacher and assembly. As we will see below, this reality is grounded in the presence of the Holy Spirit, given in baptism, to both preacher and members of the assembly.

When the preacher turns to address the assembly, the difference necessary for human communication becomes clear. To speak in one's own voice, from one's own experience of encounter with the word of God, is to reveal the human as well as the divine. As Robert Todd Townshend puts it, when the scriptural word is preached in the liturgical context, "the goal is to open and maintain a space in the hearing of the church where the Holy Spirit can do what the Spirit wills."[43] The "space" which is opened here is a space of difference—the difference between the preacher and the assembly and ultimately between the Spirit and the gathered community of preacher and assembly. In this context, the unifying presence of the Spirit is found not in the words of the preacher or in the response of the assembly, but rather in the relationship between them. As Deborah

43. Robert Todd Townshend, *The Sacramentality of Preaching: Homiletic Uses of Louis-Marie Chauvet's Theology of Sacramentality*, American University Studies (New York: Peter Lang, 2009), 118.

Organ observes, the homily "does not impart something that the community does not already know; rather it recalls and touches what is already deep within."[44] The focus is not on the words of the preacher teaching something to the assembly, but on that which is evoked in preacher and assembly through the preaching event. That which is "deep within" may be the shared life and memories of the assembly, who have been formed by the paschal mystery since their baptisms. It could also be understood as the presence of the Holy Spirit, given at their baptisms and active in the thoughts, words, and actions of both preacher and assembly. Most fundamentally, the homily is not about the transfer of new information, but about opening a space so that the presence of the Spirit can be recognized and accepted once again. Through the preaching event, the community discovers within itself that which is completely familiar and known, and which is simultaneously *different* from who they may have thought they were before the preaching encounter.

In this realization, the community also begins to recognize the difference between itself as a human community and the presence of the Spirit in its midst. Again, the difference is not one of separation but of unity in relationship. In the preaching event, "[t]he *Pneuma,* evoking in us the response of faith[,] affords us accessibility to the Word—so that it is now the Father's Word uttered *in us.*"[45] In the difference between the human words of the preacher and the divine presence of the Holy Spirit, the human response of faith, evoked in the space necessary for relationship, transforms the gathered assembly into not only hearers but also bearers of the word of God. They become one with the word of God uttered to them and now in them. The necessary difference has been transformed into unity.

When preaching is at its best and a real relationship is built in the difference between preacher and assembly, the space which opens can crackle with the presence of the Holy Spirit. Whether comforted or provoked, assemblies can often identify a preacher or a homily whose words open within them a place of transformation. In some cases, however,

44. Deborah A. Organ, "Enkindling Fire in and among Us: An Operative Theology of Liturgical Preaching," *Liturgical Ministry* 15 (Winter 2006): 12–13.

45. William Hill, *Search for the Absent God: Tradition and Modernity in Religious Understanding* (New York: Crossroad, 1992), 168.

the presence of the Holy Spirit in the midst of a preaching event can be difficult to detect. Perhaps the assembly is lethargic or preoccupied. The preacher may be having an "off" day or may have lacked the necessary time to prepare. Such experiences, especially if frequent, can be damaging both to communities and to individuals. They do not necessarily, however, indicate a complete absence of the Holy Spirit. As Craig Satterlee notes in the context of his work on the fourth-century preaching of Ambrose of Milan, "we must acknowledge the impossibility of documenting the presence and activity of the Holy Spirit which is vital to sermon preparation and gives life to the preaching event."[46] Even in the work of a renowned preacher such as Ambrose, the presence of the Holy Spirit, while presumed, cannot be documented or pinpointed in either the preparation or in the event itself. The place of the Spirit is in the differences between preacher and assembly and between preparation and life. It may also be in the difference between what is and what might have been.

The occasional mediocre preaching event, in which the presider is unprepared or the assembly is distracted, is one experience. But occasionally, the event may be experienced as worse than mediocre. Mary Catherine Hilkert points out that recognition of the gift of the Spirit given to all Christians in their baptisms can become central to discerning the work of the Spirit, even in the experience of preaching which seems significantly less than inspired. "When living in fidelity to its baptismal vocation, the Christian assembly knows when it has not heard the word of God, [or] when the proclamation of the reign of God is absent, manipulated, or distorted."[47] Such a recognition emerges out of a community which recognizes the Spirit in the points of intersection within their own human relationships, and has already, as Chauvet puts it, found God in these places "in between."[48] Such a community, which has offered their

46. Craig Alan Satterlee, *Ambrose of Milan's Method of Mystagogical Preaching* (Collegeville, MN: Liturgical Press, 2002), 18. William Hill notes that "[g]enuine preaching occurs only when the Holy Spirit (in St. Paul's phrase) 'lays fast hold upon' the faith-consciousness of the one called to preach. But the Spirit is invisible, intangible, ineffable." Hill, *Search for the Absent God*, 169.

47. Mary Catherine Hilkert, *Naming Grace: Preaching and the Sacramental Imagination* (New York: Continuum, 1997), 85.

48. Chauvet, *Symbol and Sacrament*, 522–32.

collective body as the place of the word of God, will be open to the working of the Holy Spirit in the assembly as well as in the preacher. As Hilkert adds, "[w]hen the gospel is not preached in a liberating way, the Spirit of God will be active in the hearers of the word, keeping open their resistance and empowering their imaginations to continue to envision the alternative vision of the reign of God."[49] Here the Holy Spirit, already present in the lives of both baptized preacher and assembly, may be perceived to act through the bodies of the assembly in order to move the community back toward its Christian identity.

Although the preacher plays a critical role in the preaching event and has a sacred obligation to prepare adequately and carefully, a pneumatological perspective on the preaching event indicates clearly that the responsibility is not solely that of the preacher. Richard Lennan observes that "faithfulness to the Spirit mandates attention to the manifold voices that can express the Spirit."[50] These voices are not only the voices of designated preachers but also the voices who respond to preachers, in relationship, moving the community toward recognition of the Spirit emerging in difference. The pneumatological perspective shifts our focus from the binary of preacher and assembly to the "third" term, which is the binding of the relationship between the two. The Holy Spirit is less visible in any one individual than in the relationships of symbolic exchange which occur among individuals and groups.

"Let Your Spirit Come upon These Gifts"[51]

After the gathered community has presented itself for transformation to become the place of what Hill calls the "Father's Word uttered *in us*,"[52]

49. Hilkert, *Naming Grace*, 85–86.

50. As Richard Lennan observes, "Since the Spirit is the source of the dynamism of tradition, faithfulness to the Spirit mandates attention to the manifold voices that can express the Spirit. This, in turn, speaks to the need for a commitment to the ongoing reception and re-reception of tradition." Richard Lennan, "The Church as a Sacrament of Hope," *Theological Studies* 72, no. 2 (2011): 266.

51. "Eucharistic Prayer II," in *The Sacramentary* (New York: Catholic Book Publishing, 1974).

52. Hill, *Search for the Absent God*, 191.

members of the assembly turn together to the ritual sacraments in which the unifying presence of the Spirit is made explicit in the epicletic prayers. These prayers, centered around the work of the Spirit in the world, draw attention to the unity of the bodies and spirits of believers in the assembly. The physical elements are blessed for the sake of the transformation of the assembly into the body of Christ, which they offer as what Chauvet calls a "return-gift." This transformation is not only individual but also corporate. Offering what some consider to be a corrective for an excessively christological understanding of the Eucharist, the pneumatological lens also illuminates the unity of presider and assembly and points toward the inherent unity of liturgy and life.

The epicletic prayers, although of christological nature in their earliest manifestations,[53] are in the contemporary context clearly associated with the presence of the Holy Spirit in history. These prayers, defined broadly as prayers "calling down the Holy Spirit upon an object—e.g., the water of baptism—to sanctify it and render it fruitful for its destined use,"[54] are found in various sacramental rituals but are heard most frequently in the eucharistic celebration. Closely associated with the institution narratives, these prayers request the transformation of the gifts of bread and wine through the power of the Holy Spirit. As John McKenna points out, in ancient sources such as the *Apostolic Tradition* and the *Anaphora of Addai and Mari,* as well as in the later commentaries of Nicholas Cabasilas, the epicletic prayers almost invariably request, "a transformation of the gifts *so that* the faithful might receive such benefits as unity, forgiveness, and life in the present and/or in the eschatological future."[55] This

53. See Michael Zheltov, "The Moment of Eucharistic Consecration in Byzantine Thought," in *Issues in Eucharistic Praying in East and West: Essays in Liturgical and Theological Analysis*, ed. Maxwell Johnson (Collegeville, MN: Liturgical Press, 2011). See also Paul Bradshaw, *Eucharistic Origins* (Oxford: Oxford University Press, 2004), 126.

54. Robert Taft, "From Logos to Spirit: On the Early History of the Epiclesis," in *Gratias Agamus: Studien Zum Eucharistischen Hochgebet*, ed. Andreas Heinz and Heinrich Rennings (Freiburg: Herder, 1992), 489. Paul Bradshaw notes that the Greek word *epiklesis*, which first appears in Christian liturgical usage in Irenaeus's *Against Heresies*, means simply 'invocation.' See Bradshaw, *Eucharistic Origins*, 93.

55. John H. McKenna, "Eucharistic Epiclesis: Myopia or Microcosm?," *Theological Studies* 36, no. 2 (1975): 266. See also McKenna, "Eucharistic Presence: An Invitation to Dialogue," *Theological Studies* 60, no. 2 (1999).

transformation, which is effected through the consecrated elements, is at the heart of what the scholastics called the *res tantum*. The elements are transformed for the sake of human beings, who in turn are transformed for the sake of the world. This sacramental approach affects both the bodies and the spirits of the participants. The transformed physical elements are consumed for the sake of spiritual transformation, which in turn becomes manifest in embodied actions in the world.

The epiclesis also highlights the unity of the praying assembly, which together with the presider, pleads that the Spirit might once again come upon their gifts of selves and elements. While recognizing that the ordained presider "does indeed have a special and ordinary function,"[56] McKenna regards the epiclesis as helpful in "counteract[ing] any tendency to exaggerate the role of the ordained minister at the expense of the whole assembly."[57] As the institution narrative tends to emphasize the christological elements of the eucharistic prayers, and may focus attention on the ordained presider who acts *in persona Christi*, the epiclesis highlights the unity of the baptized who together invoke the Spirit's intervention. This offers a corrective to what Robert Daly has criticized as a "lack of trinitiarian perspective and massive overemphasis on the christological perspective," which corresponds to a "neglect of the role of the participating faithful."[58] Here the epicletic prayers serve to highlight the unity of assembly and presider as they await the work of the Holy Spirit in the space between themselves and God's work on their behalf.

Finally, the restoration of the epicletic prayers in the Western rites itself functions as a renewed sign of increasing ecumenical unity. As E. Byron Anderson points out, even in the modern ecumenical context, churches

56. McKenna, "Eucharistic Epiclesis: Myopia or Microcosm?," 272.

57. Ibid. Edward Kilmartin suggests that when the words of institution become isolated, the christological dimension can be emphasized "to the neglect or exclusion of the ecclesiological. . . . In other words, the liturgical assembly of the Christian faithful seems merely to provide the proper context of the celebration of the Eucharist, rather than being the active subject of the celebration itself." Edward Kilmartin, *The Eucharist in the West: History and Theology* (Collegeville, MN: Liturgical Press, 1998), 347. See also 348–51. See also Patrick Regan, "Quenching the Spirit: The Epiclesis in Recent Roman Documents," *Worship* 79, no. 5 (2005).

58. Robert Daly, "Robert Bellarmine and Post-Tridentine Eucharistic Theology," *Theological Studies* 61, no. 2 (2000): 259. Ibid., 240.

have tended to focus on "questions of institution and consecration"[59] rather than on the bigger picture of the role of the Holy Spirit in the overarching eucharistic celebration. The prayers of epiclesis move Western churches closer to the eucharistic theologies of their Eastern counterparts, thus illuminating the role of the Holy Spirit in the process of ecumenical liturgical unity.

From Pew to Parking Lot and Beyond

The role of the Spirit, present in the difference between God and humanity and between human beings as individuals and in liturgical roles, also frames the relationship between what *Sacrosanctum Concilium* calls "the two parts of the liturgy," which form "one single act of worship" (SC 56). When Chauvet's pneumatological understanding of the system of symbolic exchange is applied to the liturgy as a whole, the inherent unity of the liturgical celebration becomes evident. Following the Faith and Order Commission's suggestion for a shift away from comparison of the "intensity of the various modes of [Christ's] presence,"[60] the unity of presence and celebration becomes clear through a three-part model which avoids the dangers of hierarchical dualism. Chauvet's "tripod"[61] of Scripture, sacrament, and ethics offers a way to reconsider the Christian experience through the transformative "marks" of Christian identity, the practice of which both shapes individual Christians and allows them to play their parts in the continuous growth of the church as the body of Christ on earth. These marks apply to all members of the Christian faithful, clergy and laity, and demonstrate that the Christian life and the liturgical celebration as a whole are best understood as aspects of the larger movement of the Holy Spirit in the created world.

Drawing on the Emmaus story in the Gospel of Luke, itself a clear articulation of the paschal mystery, Chauvet sketches what he understands to be the proper relationship between these three formative elements of

59. E. Byron Anderson, "A Body in the Spirit for the World: Eucharist, Epiclesis, and Ethics," *Worship* 85, no. 2 (2011): 99.

60. Günther Gassmann, *Documentary History of Faith and Order, 1963–1993*, Faith and Order Paper no. 159 (Geneva: WCC Publications, 1993), 12.

61. Ibid., 176.

Christian identity.[62] In retelling the story, Chauvet reflects first on the experience of the disciples on the road to Emmaus who were instructed on the Scriptures by a stranger. Although they do not hear the *Scriptures* proclaimed from a book, they receive instruction and interpretation from the mouth of Jesus himself, who goes unrecognized until he says the blessing and breaks the bread. In this *sacramental* moment of fracture and transformation, Jesus disappears from sight, and the disciples are drawn into *ethical action* as proclaimers of the word of faith in history. It is the role of the Holy Spirit, especially in the points of relationship within these "marks," which binds them together in difference and makes a coherent whole of a liturgy which might otherwise be considered to consist of two parts.

Following the structure set by the Emmaus story, Chauvet begins with a discussion of the received word of the Bible and other Christian texts. By "Scripture" he means

> everything that pertains to the *knowledge* of God's mystery revealed in Jesus Christ: the Bible in the first place of course, since it contains all the foundational texts of the church's faith; but also all the theological discourse of yesterday and today, because theology is at bottom nothing else than the orderly and critically organized elucidation of the difficulties present in our foundational texts. Catechesis belongs also.[63]

The term "Scripture" thus pertains to the words and texts received as gift from God and built up by earlier members of the Christian community. Both divine and human contributions are acknowledged. Like the other elements of the structure, the Scriptures do not give immediate access to God. The difference between God and humanity, the fruitful place of the Spirit, must be maintained.[64] The Scriptures thus mediate God's presence

62. Ibid., 161–70.

63. Chauvet, *The Sacraments*, 29.

64. Chauvet insists that the formality of liturgical ritual is itself helpful in maintaining this distinction. Although he believes that the liturgical rites should be comprehensible to participants, he regards the formality of ritual as a helpful reminder that "as near as God has become to human beings in Jesus, God demands to be treated with respect . . . the words of the liturgy, even if they come from common speech, yet do not belong to it, point to this communication in and by the means

through the word, in physical absence. Christians accept this gift of God's mediated presence, which is beyond value, and enter into the dialogue. Their response is the sacraments, another divine and human endeavor offered to humanity by God in history and now sustained in history by the work of the Holy Spirit.

In the context of the sacraments, Chauvet emphasizes the role of the Holy Spirit as active in history, transforming believers as they encounter God's presence and absence in the sacraments. Since the notion of sacrament is closely connected to the offering of thanksgiving to God (the return gift offered in thanksgiving for God's self-revelation in the Scriptures),[65] Chauvet defines the sacraments broadly as "everything that has to do with the celebration of the Triune God in the *liturgy*."[66] The liturgical celebration of the sacraments thus encompasses the proclamation and preaching of Scripture as well as the ritual prayers structured around word and element. Although sacraments tend to be associated with their physical elements, Chauvet emphasizes that "every sacrament is a sacrament of the word—the live word brought to us by the Holy Spirit."[67] Here, the word of God is "mediated under the ritual mode, different from the mode of Scripture,"[68] yet is still revelatory and sacramental. Christians living in history after the physical death of Jesus, Chauvet insists, must consciously renounce a search for the physical body of Christ (which is risen and absent) and "[c]onsent to his symbolic body of the word, which is the Church."[69] They do this by accepting that God's presence is always mediated by the three elements of Christian identity and by the larger community of the church, guided by the Holy Spirit, practicing the symbolic exchange of these elements.

In both Scripture and sacrament, Chauvet argues for a more holistic understanding of the work of the Spirit in the space of *difference* between physical and sacramental presence. "The Spirit is God as *ungraspable,*

---

of distance." Chauvet, "Are the Words of the Liturgy Worn Out? What Diagnosis? What Pastoral Approach?," *Worship* 84, no. 1 (2010): 32.

65. Chauvet, *The Sacraments*, 30.

66. Chauvet, *Symbol and Sacrament*, 170.

67. Chauvet, *The Sacraments*, 93.

68. Ibid., 48.

69. Chauvet, *Symbol and Sacrament*, 173.

always-surprising, always-elusive; it is the God who cannot be managed, continually spilling over every religious institution."[70] While the Scripture and the sacraments can be understood as different "modes" of God's presence, the Spirit is present in both and in the relationship between them. Thus the sacraments are always "sacraments of the Word in the Spirit."[71] As Christians move from the experience of the Scriptures to the celebration of the sacraments, they encounter the "ungraspable" Spirit of God who eludes categories and brings unity from difference both in what *Sacrosanctum Concilium* calls the "two parts" of the liturgy and in the points of difference, but not separation, between liturgical celebration and the rest of Christian life.

As with the breaking of the bread in the Emmaus story, the sacraments operate in the liturgy as a point of transformation that leads to embodied action. In the inn along the road to Emmaus, the breaking of the bread functions as a moment of transformative insight and simultaneous loss. Having had the Scriptures explained to them, the disciples watch the risen Christ perform an action that echoed many of the prophetic food miracles undertaken during his earthly life. When the bread is broken, the risen Christ disappears from their presence, leaving them with an absence which they can now identify. This absence, or space between longing and reality, is the place of the Christian life lived in the sacramental presence of Christ. Like the disciples who promptly returned to proclaim the word in Jerusalem, through the working of the Spirit in this place of sacramental openness, "in the sacraments, the believers' bodies absorb the word heard in the Scriptures in order to transform it into life."[72] This transformation, mediated by the word that is given, finds a necessarily physical form in the ethical actions of individuals.

Like Scripture and sacrament, ethical action is ultimately also an expression of the word of God written on the bodies of human beings by the Holy Spirit. Chauvet writes: "Under the paradigm 'ethics' we place all that pertains to *action* in the name of the gospel (therefore also, and even primarily, in the name of humanity)."[73] Although the sacramental

70. Ibid., 513.
71. Ibid., 221.
72. Chauvet, *The Sacraments*, 147.
73. Ibid., 31.

ritual, performed according to the rite that has been given to the church, is one form of return offering, Chauvet observes that

> the "we offer you" of the anamnesis is not a simple declarative or informative sentence, but a language act that is self-implicative . . . to become historically and eschatologically the body of him whom they are offering sacramentally, the members of the assembly are committed to live out their own oblation of themselves in self-giving to others as Christ did.[74]

It is in ethical action, as a response to the transformation that happens in the sacrament, that Christians both acknowledge the absence of Christ and, "being the place where the book of the Spirit is written, thus become a living word revealing Christ"[75] in their own historical milieu. In their own language and interactions, they take on the identity of the body of the absent Christ in the world. "The place of the theological is the anthropological,"[76] and the relationship is always mediated by a word which is, as Chauvet puts it, "at the mercy of the body."[77] Through this third mode of the word, Chauvet makes the connection between liturgical action and the human role in maintaining the sacramentality of the world. The transforming liturgical action bears fruit in ethical action in which the word of Christ is embodied in those who seek to make the world a welcoming place for everyone.[78] In these ethical actions, Christians contribute to the sacramentality of the world, and also continue to be formed in their own Christian identity as they renounce the quest to seek the physical Christ in the world and allow themselves to be shaped by the Spirit at work in the words and deeds of their neighbors.

Chauvet's understanding of the unity of the liturgical celebration itself and its unitive relationship with the rest of the Christian life is rooted in an understanding of "modes" of the word of God which are facilitated by the Holy Spirit through relationships of symbolic exchange in history. When the Spirit "writes the letter of the Scriptures in the hearts of believers"[79] and

74. Chauvet, *Symbol and Sacrament*, 277. It is here that the return-gift of gratitude is "verified" in ethical action.

75. Chauvet, *The Sacraments*, 65.

76. Ibid.

77. Ibid., xii.

78. Chauvet, *Symbol and Sacrament*, 553.

79. Chauvet, *The Sacraments*, 166.

"appears as the agent of God's embodiment: it gives a body to the Word,"[80] first in the very body of Christ, and later in the church.[81] Thus the preached word, the epicletic word, and the word proclaimed in ethical choices made in everyday life for the sake of participation in the paschal mystery are all elements of the same movement. The differences in relationship between these moments are points of connection in the Holy Spirit, uniting believers around the "one table" which extends from the pews to the parking lot and beyond.

The lens of pneumatology is thus helpful for understanding the unity of the liturgical action as well as the integral unity between the liturgical celebration and the everyday lives of the Christian faithful. Attention to the pneumatic elements of the liturgy, particularly the preaching event and the epicletic prayers, illustrates the work of the Spirit at points of relational difference. Although this presence of the Spirit is, as Hill puts it, "invisible, intangible, ineffable,"[82] it becomes manifest in the relational *difference* between divine and human, presider and assembly, Scripture and sacrament. In the epiclesis, the community gathers as one as the presider leads the assembly in a prayer for the Spirit's transformative presence. In the more dialogical preaching context, the Spirit can be found in the space between the words of the preacher and the active participation of the baptized assembly. These particular liturgical elements serve as landmarks[83] for the work of the Holy Spirit in the overarching liturgical context, eventually expanding from the transformative liturgical moments to the transformed and transformative life of the Christian. At every point, it is the task of the whole person, body and spirit, to offer herself for transformation, both for her own sake and for the sake of the world.

80. Ibid.

81. David Power observes, "it is to the Spirit that [Chauvet] attributes . . . the capacity for the Word to take body in the Church." David N. Power, "The Word in the Liturgy: Incarnating the Gospel in Cultures," in *Sacraments: Revelation of the Humanity of God: Engaging the Fundamental Theology of Louis-Marie Chauvet*, ed. Phillippe Bordeyne and Bruce T. Morrill (Collegeville, MN: Liturgical Press, 2008), 60. See also: Chauvet, *Symbol and Sacrament*, 526–27.

82. Hill, *Search for the Absent God*, 169.

83. See Karl Rahner, "Considerations on the Active Role of the Person in the Sacramental Event," in *Theological Investigations 14* (New York: Crossroad, 1983), 169.

Conclusion: "And [Also] with Your Spirit"

"And [also] with your spirit." What theology is the assembly working out for itself as individuals stumble on unfamiliar words for ancient ideas? As Chauvet has argued, and experience confirms, there is no lack of dualism in the world today. Cable news anchors portray red states against blue states. Individuals report that they are "spiritual, but not religious." Catholic bloggers on the right and left attack each other with great energy. In the midst of all of this, the temptation to separate the bodily from the spiritual, the mundane from the sublime, is strong. It is tempting to think that one addresses the pure spirit of the presider to imply, perhaps, that his embodied actions are of less consequence than his elevated spirit. As Chauvet also points out, to wish for this is perhaps natural, but to achieve it is neither realistic nor entirely desirable. Sacramental theology insists that God comes to humanity in the mundane elements of our daily existence, through new language and old language, through self and neighbor, through the liturgy of the church and the liturgy of the world. The pneumatological lens invites us to look for points of intersection in difference and to see unifying relationships rather than separation.

In attending to the work of the Holy Spirit in the liturgy, it becomes clear that the primary point of difference in which the Spirit may be found is not necessarily the homiletic or creedal bridge between the Liturgy of the Word and the Liturgy of the Eucharist. To some degree, this point is not emphasized because the work of the Spirit is clearly found in both "parts" of the liturgy. In the points of difference between original event and ritual remembrance, preacher and assembly, bread and body, the work of the Spirit is woven throughout the liturgy, orienting believers toward the third mark of Christian identity which is exercised in the world. In addition to illuminating the unity of the liturgical celebration itself and the unity of celebration and life, the pneumatological lens also sheds light on the significance of liturgical embodiment, especially as it pertains to the unity that can emerge from diversity both in the assembly and in the larger community which comprises the assembly.

As Chauvet reminds us, it is through "I-bodies" that human beings are able to maintain the identity in difference which is necessary for relationship. In this context, it is possible to experience the presider's greeting as a gift offered from one "I-body" to another. As presider and assembly address one another, seeing neither an outside shell nor a disembodied spirit, they can recognize in each other "the primordial place of every symbolic joining of the 'inside' and the 'outside' "[84] Coming into understanding of ourselves in the midst of culture and tradition, Christians are never isolated individuals reducible merely to bodies or spirits. This acceptance of embodiment as the condition for unifying relationship is at the heart of the reason for physically gathering for the liturgical celebration. A televised Mass may provide a more "spiritual" relationship, but it does not allow for the work of the Holy Spirit in the physical presence of other "I-bodies" who make up the assembly on any given Sunday morning. The work of the Holy Spirit, present in the realization of difference and connection between these "I-bodies," binds the community together not only as the body of Christ but also as friends, family members, and neighbors who relate to one another "in the Spirit" whether they are in the church building or elsewhere. Without the presence of "I-bodies" in the assembly, however, the starting point for these relationships is missing.

In addition to the opportunity for human relationships which develop within difference, the presence of the "I-bodies" also indicates the reality of spiritual transformation effected through material elements. Building on the recognition of the unity of body and soul which makes relationships possible, the epicletic prayers to the Holy Spirit both address the physical and spiritual needs of the community through sacramental food and point to the unity between individual transformation and transformation of the world for the sake of the kingdom of God. The outward focus of the epiclesis emphasizes that the gifts are transformed for the sake of human transformation, and that human transformation is effected for the sake of the transformation of the world. Here the sacraments are understood not as ends in themselves but as transitional moments in which losses are mourned and new challenges are accepted. As with the Emmaus disciples, a modern Christian's awareness of loss can bring both transformation and clarity about one's mission. A pneumatological lens encourages Christians to pivot from the ritual celebration of thanksgiving to the ongoing celebration in which one verifies thanksgiving through ethical action.

Finally, the pneumatological lens offers the reminder that differences and diversity are both the place of the Spirit and the source of unity in

84. Chauvet, *Symbol and Sacrament*, 150.

relationship. Diverse roles, diverse backgrounds, diverse approaches to problem solving exist and cause tension in all communities. These differences also present new opportunities to look for the presence of the Spirit, building unity in relationships which may, at first glance, appear to be grounded in differences of separation rather than points of intersection. When a community living in the Spirit that was bestowed on each individual at baptism looks carefully at their relationships, they may find that which is familiar and which they have always known, even in points of heated disagreement. When recognized, these places of the Spirit can strengthen a community rather than fracture it.

"And *also* with your Spirit." Although the transitional phrase will soon be forgotten, the "also" highlights a theological instinct toward unity which emerged from assemblies during a time of tension, change, and disagreement. The Spirit, the bringer of unity in difference, is present in the difference between new words and old words, presider and assembly, in the binding of spirit and body in human "I-bodies," and in the symbolic joining of "inside" and "outside" when an individual begins to encounter and find her place in the world. Disrupting dualism, the Spirit spans the whole of liturgy and life, weaving together difference and uniting Christians around the one table.

chapter 3

Transformative Unity

The Language of Liturgy in Word and Sacrament

When the lector ascends to the ambo and draws a breath to begin the proclamation, when the priest begins the institution narrative with the familiar words, "at the time he was betrayed and entered willingly into his Passion,"[1] the realities of human language and divine language, spoken and written word, authorship, readership, and hearership are all madly colliding in the sanctuary. Somewhere in the midst of this cacophony, Christians claim to hear "the still small voice of God" (1 Kgs 19:12) speaking to their hearts. Stories are told and transformation is effected. Yet the words, clear though they may sound, slip away from us. Do we hear the voice of God or the lector? How do spoken symbols have the power to transform? How can the lens of language illustrate the inherent unity of the "one table of the word of God and Body of Christ" (DV 21) as experienced in the eucharistic liturgy?

The Judeo-Christian tradition has much to say about language as mediator for the presence of God. The idea of the *logos* or "word" of God itself precedes the Christian tradition and is indicative of an early association

1. "Eucharistic Prayer II," in *A Commentary on the Order of Mass of The Roman Missal: A New English Translation*, ed. Edward Foley, et al. (Collegeville, MN: Liturgical Press, 2011), 305.

between language and God's presence. In the first century of the Common Era, figures such as Philo of Alexandria (a possible influence on John the Evangelist), developed a theology of language which emphasized that God's language was both personal and powerful; it was capable of transforming both people and things, and in most cases, it required mediation. As Philo pointed out, the Scriptures themselves are a form of this mediation and are not the literal "word of the Lord." When later Christians began to reflect on the theology of the emerging sacraments, building on the logos Christology which was already developing, they chose to do so in terms of language. Augustine's sacramental theology is rooted in his understanding of the ways that language functions in relationships. Interpreting the linguistic signs found in Scripture and sacrament, his work points to the transformative power of language, grounded in trinitarian relationships, both in the entirety of the liturgical context and outside of it. In our contemporary context, biblicists and theologians (now distinct categories in a way that would have made little sense to Philo or Augustine) have begun to address the complexities and insights that emerge from our habit of applying the same word "language" to divine and human self-communication. Arguing from the perspective that grace builds on nature, Karl Rahner explores the many ways that grace is mediated in the form of the word. Rahner and other modern and postmodern theologians emphasize the relational qualities of language, observing that to refer to God's self-communication as "language" or "word" is to speak in metaphors for something that we can never fully understand.

When applied to God's self-communication, the metaphor of language ultimately indicates the point of encounter between God and humanity in the context of communication. This communication may take a variety of forms. As David Power helpfully points out, even human language is "not restricted to the verbal, but refers to all human media of encounter and exchange, bodily and ritual, as well as verbal."[2] In the postmodern context, Nathan Mitchell defines language as "that whole complex, interactive system of communications, verbal and nonverbal,

2. David N. Power, "Sacrament: Event Eventing," in *A Promise of Presence*, ed. Michael Downey and Richard Fragomeni (Washington, DC: The Pastoral Press, 1992), 59.

by which we become available to one another in both our embodied flesh and our interiority."[3] These definitions, emphasizing as they do the nonverbal, embodied, and ritual elements of language, open up possibilities for speaking of language as mode of communication between God and humanity. When applying this term, it is important to remember that while language may be a definitively helpful metaphor for speaking of the divine self-communication, its meaning, like the Holy Spirit, overflows conventional categories in every time and place.

To consider the unity of word and sacrament in the context of language, we turn first to Philo of Alexandria, whose theology of language became foundational for the infant Christian tradition. Philo's emphases on the personal and powerful nature of divine language laid the groundwork for a Christian understanding of the transformative power of the word of God mediated through the logos, the Scriptures, and their interpreters. We will then turn to the fifth-century bishop and rhetorician Augustine of Hippo, whose sacramental theology has grounded the work of nearly all subsequent Western sacramental theologians. Finally, we will return to contemporary Roman Catholic theologies of language which have informed late twentieth and early twenty-first-century sacramental theologies.

Philo's Theology of Language: Personal, Transformative, and Visual

In turning our attention to a first-century Jewish theology of language, we acknowledge Christian theology's debt to the Jewish and Hellenistic philosophies that came before it. Philo of Alexandria, a first-century exegete and theologian of language, developed ideas which came before him in the Jewish and Hellenistic traditions. His understanding of the logos of God, a kind of "second deity . . . the Word of the supreme Being,"[4] offers insight into the personal and creative powers that were associated

3. Nathan Mitchell, "But Only Say the Word," *Worship* 80, no. 5 (2006): 459.

4. Philo, "Questions and Answers on Genesis," in *The Works of Philo: Complete and Unabridged* (Peabody, MA: Hendrickson, 1993), 2.62; see also Philo, "Allegorical Interpretation," in *The Works of Philo*, 3.175., in which Philo states "the word of God is over all the world, and is the most ancient, and the most universal of all the things that are created."

with divine language in the first century and that are referenced in the Prologue to the Gospel of John. Philo understands the power of divine language to be so great as to require mediation in order for human beings to experience it without harm. This mediation takes a variety of forms, some of them visible. Even in its mediated state, divine language retains its transformative and creative power. Human beings are changed by their experience of it, much in the way that later Christians would suggest that they are transformed by the sacraments. We turn first to the concept of *logos*, literally the "word." Central to the Christian tradition, the idea of logos has its roots in Hellenistic philosophy and in Second Temple Jewish scriptural interpretation. Philo develops this concept in the context of a theology of language, emphasizing the role of language as mediator of revelation.

Long associated with the larger concept of language, the term *logos* can be dated as early as Heraclitus in the fifth century BCE. In these early instances, Heraclitus thought of logos as a means to express continuity and order in the midst of the visible chaos of the universe.[5] Continuing to develop in Platonic, Stoic, and Jewish philosophy, the term retained connotations of language, reason, and order.[6] Working from the Greek Septuagint text of the Old Testament, which referred to God's speech as logos, Philo expanded the concept in the Jewish tradition and suggested "that the Logos represents the archetypal speech of God which is copied and embodied in the physical universe."[7] In this argument we hear an echo of the Platonic idea of the created world as a kind of copy of the ideal world. Here human language is understood as the created imitation of divine language which, like God, is uncreated.[8] While human language is "divided into nouns and verbs, and in short into all the different parts of

5. Raymond Brown, *The Gospel According to John I–XII*, ed. William Foxwell Albright and David Noel Freedman, vol. 29, The Anchor Bible (Garden City, NY: Doubleday, 1964), 520.

6. See especially Plato, *Timaeus*.

7. David Winston, *Logos and Mystical Theology in Philo of Alexandria* (Cincinnati: Hebrew Union College Press, 1985), 15–19.

8. See also Maren R. Niehoff, "What Is in a Name? Philo's Mystical Philosophy of Language," *Jewish Studies Quarterly* 2, no. 2 (1995): 224–26.

speech,"[9] divine language, signaled by the use of the term *logos*, is simple and perfect.

For Philo, this ideal language provides the manner in which both reason and divine revelation can become available to humanity. Divine language is "comparable to the radiance of light and a fountain of reason,"[10] which illuminates human life experience through stimulation of human reason. Philo describes this intense experience of revelation using a variety of metaphors including light, water, and the planting of seeds. He writes:

> sometimes when I have come to my work empty I have suddenly become full, ideas being, in an invisible manner, showered upon me, and implanted in me from on high; so that, through the influence of divine inspiration, I have become greatly excited, and have known neither the place in which I was nor those who were present, nor myself, nor what I was saying, nor what I was writing; for then I have been conscious of a richness of interpretation, an enjoyment of light, a most penetrating sight, a most manifest energy in all that was to be done, having such an effect on my mind as the clearest ocular demonstration would have on the eyes. (*Migration* 1.35)

This stimulation is described in terms of a metaphysical change that adapts the human capacity to receive divine revelation. As Philo describes it, ideas that did not exist before are showered on or implanted in his mind, leaving him in an altered state. Although the difference between human beings and divine beings would make it naturally impossible for communication to occur, God's transformative word shapes human beings so that they become capable of receiving super-natural revelation. As David Winston explains, "in spite of the earthly mind's denied access to *the* divine essence, as an imprint or effulgence of the Logos, it enjoys the happiness and blessedness that consciousness of its high spiritual estate bestows upon it."[11] The human mind is rational because it was created by

9. Philo, "On the Migration of Abraham," in *The Works of Philo*, 1.48.

10. Niehoff, "What Is in a Name?," 224. These images for divine language will emerge later as Philo develops his understanding of divine language, or the *logos* of God "as a Divine emanation which is expressed in the creation of the world." Ibid., 221.

11. David Winston, "Philo's Linguistic Theory," in *Heirs of the Septuagint: Philo, Hellenistic Judaism and Early Christianity: Festschrift for Earl Hilgert*, ed. David Runia,

and modeled on the divine reason of the logos. This rationality provides the grounds for the possibility of receiving divine revelation.

When human beings encounter the logos or word of God, their minds are shaped by the knowledge of God, which, of course, is also the knowledge that brought about their own initial embodied creation by means of God's creative speech acts described in Genesis. As Philo puts it,

> Having considered that the knowledge of the Creator and the proper understanding of the work of Creation, would be of great advantage to the creature . . . [God] breathed into him from above something of his own divine nature. And his divine nature stamped her own impression in an invisible manner on the invisible soul, in order that even the earth might not be destitute of the image of God.[12]

Maren Niehoff points out that Philo is the first to apply the allegory of a stamp or seal to the effects of divine language.[13] For Philo, it is this divine stamp, originating from creation, which creates the link between God and humanity, and makes it possible for communication to take place. The seal is indicative of the creative and, by extension, transformative potential of language, both divine and human.

The connection between human language and the image of God is directly related to the fact that divine language is most often mediated through human beings who, while bearing the image of God, also speak in human language. For Philo, the mediated experience of God's revelation often takes visible form. In rare cases this is because the divine language itself is more appropriately seen than heard. In more normal cases, it is because most human beings will experience divine revelation through the words, symbols, writings, and gestures of other human beings. We turn first to Philo's understanding of the rare but significant occasions on which human beings see, rather than hear, the language of God. We will then turn to the more common instances in which some human beings mediate revelation to others.

David Hay, and David Winston, The Studia Philonica Annual III, Brown Judaic Studies (Atlanta: Scholar's Press, 1991), 123.

12. Philo, "That the Worse Attacks the Better," in *The Works of Philo*, 1.86.

13. Niehoff, "What Is in a Name?," 243.

One of the touchstones in Philo's theology of language is the Exodus account of the theophany on Sinai. In this account we find a group theophany in which the people respond with fear and concern regarding exposure to the voice of God. According to the modern translation of the New American Bible, this passage would seem to represent the more usual category of mediated revelation. "Now as all the people witnessed the thunder and lightning, the blast of the shofar and the mountain smoking, they became afraid and trembled. So they took up a position farther away" (Exod 20:18-19). The people are concerned that if they have a direct encounter with the voice of God, it will mean their deaths. They instead request that Moses act as the mediator between themselves and the direct experience of God. While the New American translation emphasizes the people's fear of encounter with the voice of God, the Septuagint text, which Philo would have used, suggests that God protected the people by offering them a vision, rather than an aural encounter. While the Hebrew of Exodus 20:18 can be understood idiomatically as "all the people witnessed the thunder," the Septuagint renders the passage in the singular according to the primary literal meaning of the words, "the whole people was seeing the voice." Rather than hearing the voice of God, according to the Septuagint, the people experienced the voice through sight; their senses could not function as usual to comprehend the unmediated encounter with God.

In the Septuagint translation, the theophany at Sinai occasions an experience of synesthesia, a "merging of seeing, hearing, smelling, tasting and touching—in a unified experience of the sacred."[14] The religious experience of theophany was so overwhelming to the people that their senses sought to make sense of the sacred through what David Chidester calls "a crossmodal transfer from seeing to hearing or hearing to seeing."[15] They saw, rather than heard, the voice of God. The crossmodal transfer between hearing and sight operates to underscore the distinction between divine and human language, and to emphasize the superiority of divine language. As Chidester points out, in the Greco-Roman world's hierarchy of the senses, the visual was normally preferred to the aural. This

14. David Chidester, *Word and Light: Seeing, Hearing, and Religious Discourse* (Urbana: University of Illinois Press, 1992), 54.

15. Ibid.

preference is clear in Philo's interpretation: "A voice sounded forth from out of the midst of the fire which had flowed from heaven, a most marvelous and awful voice, the flame being endowed with articulate speech in a language familiar to the hearers, which expressed its words with such clearness and distinctness that the people seemed rather to be seeing than hearing it. And the law testifies to the accuracy of my statement, where it is written, 'And all the people beheld the voice most evidently.' "[16] As Philo understands it, the flame itself is "endowed with articulate speech" so that the people "see" the voice of God. Associating the voice of God with visible light, Philo further elevates the significance of the event, insisting that the Scriptures "do not say, 'heard it,' since what took place was not a beating of the air by means of the organs of the mouth and tongue, but a most exceedingly brilliant ray of virtue, not different in any respect from the source of reason" (*Migration* 1.47).[17] Philo's reference to the "source of reason" indicates that the visual ray both originates with, and in fact *is*, the logos or word of God, which is for Philo the source of human reason. It thus expresses itself, with Platonic simplicity, in the visual experience rather than discretely in the nouns, verbs, and other parts of speech employed by human language.[18]

16. Philo, "On the Decalogue," in *The Works of Philo*, 1.46–47.

17. Philo's understanding of sensory perception reflects the Greco-Roman theory that human sight is facilitated by a "visual ray" emitted by the human eye which strikes an object and conveys information to the mind through its union with the object. This more active mode of sensory perception was preferred to the more passive experience of hearing, which occurred when something outside of the body produced a shock which fragmented the air; the air fragments then struck the passive ear, resulting in the reception of information. Chidester, *Word and Light: Seeing, Hearing, and Religious Discourse*, 4–8, 32–33. As Chidester notes, citing *On the Sacrifices of Cain and Abel* 78, elsewhere Philo states that "wisdom 'makes us spectators rather than hearers of knowledge, and substituted in our minds sight, the swiftest of the senses, for the slower sense of hearing.' Having achieved the insight of Wisdom, 'it is idle any longer to exercise the ear with words.'" Ibid., 33–34.

18. Philo points out that Moses speaks "with excessive precision; for the discourse which was divided into nouns and verbs, and in short into all the different parts of speech, he has very appropriately spoken of as something to be heard; for in fact that is examined by the sense of hearing; but that which has nothing to do with either nouns or verbs, but is the voice of God, and seen by the eye of the soul, he very

Like the people who asked Moses to mediate for them, Philo is aware that most human beings will experience divine revelation through the words, symbols, and gestures of other human beings. In one of the many metaphors which Philo uses to describe the ways in which divine language becomes available to human beings, he speaks of the divine word being "like a river, [which] flows forth from wisdom as from a spring, in order to irrigate and fertilize the celestial and heavenly shoots and plants of such souls as love virtue, as if they were a paradise."[19] As Niehoff puts it, when this divine language "flows into the human soul . . . it is conceived as both words and doctrines, thus implying a transformation of the ethereal and absolute into specific and humanly graspable units."[20] These "graspable units" are then passed on to other human beings in their own languages and cultures.

This act of transmission, which can take oral or written form, is the ordinary process by which most human beings encounter the word of God. Philo especially privileges the way that language functions in the Scriptures, referring to the letters of Scripture as "the minutest seal[s] which accurately display the impression of the larger figures of divine language."[21] The translation of divine revelation to human language is never, however, an easy process. Philo discusses the challenge which this process presents through the example of the work which Moses and Aaron did to convey divine revelation to the people. Speaking first of divine revelation, Philo writes,

> for when the mind being excited towards any object connected with it receives an impetus . . . it then becomes pregnant and labors to bring forth its conceptions. And, though it tries to deliver itself of them, it is unable to do so till sound, like a midwife, acting either through the

---

properly represents as visible" (*Migration* 1.48). Philo distinguishes here between human language, which is composite, and the simplicity of divine language.

19. Philo, "On Dreams," in *The Works of Philo*, 2.242.

20. Niehoff, "What Is in a Name?," 230–31. See Philo's *Posterity* 127–29 and *On the Sacrifices of Cain and Abel [Sacrifices]*, 131. Niehoff adds that "the human mind fulfills an intermediary function, translating ethereal notions into concrete words." Ibid., 227.

21. See Philo, "On the Creation of the World," 4–6, and Niehoff, "What Is in a Name?," 245–46.

> medium of the tongue or of some other of the organs of speech, receives those conceptions and brings them to light. And this voice is itself the most manifest of all the conceptions. For, as what is laid up is hidden in darkness until light shines upon it and exhibits it, in the same manner the conceptions are stored away in an invisible place, namely, the mind, until the voice, like light, sheds its beams upon them and reveals everything. (*Worse* 1.127–28)[22]

Here God's revelation excites the human mind and creates something new within it. The human voice must then act to reveal the divine mysteries that have flowed into one human soul and have become imprinted on the human mind. The divine and the created operate together here. The divine seal shapes, but does not break, the natural human mind. Without the divine imprint there is nothing to be revealed. Without the human voice or human language, revelation remains hidden from humanity.

The metaphor of gestation and childbirth speaks both to the difficulty of the process and to the mystery of that which is hidden away. Philo, like most interpreters of Platonic thought, is not entirely positive about human language as medium for the divine word. He is concerned both about loss of meaning and about the static quality of the textual word which, in contrast to the spoken word, does not allow the reader opportunity for clarification or "cross examination."[23] Due to the difference between divine and human language, however, Philo acknowledges that mediation must be accepted. As Niehoff points out, for Philo, "it is . . . the prophetic poet's word which can leave the most accurate and ethereal impression on the wax-like soul of the reader, thus creatively shaping his spiritual constitution."[24] This mediation comes through the human authors of the Bible and through interpreters, such as Philo himself, who work to make the meaning of revelation available to other human beings. The work of these scholars has an effect similar to that of God's revelation. Both leave an impression on the soul of the reader, leaving her spiritually changed and marked by the experience.

22. See also Niehoff, "What Is in a Name?," 237.
23. Winston, "Philo's Linguistic Theory," 124–25.
24. Niehoff, "What Is in a Name?," 246. See *Creation* 4–6.

Philo's understanding of divine language, the logos of God, is the foundation for logos Christology, the beginnings of which will develop early in the Christian tradition. Although there is no developed theology of language in first-century Christianity, some scholars suggest intersections between the work of Philo and the work of John the Evangelist. As Thomas Tobin puts it, "while one cannot argue that the author of the hymn in the Prologue [of the Gospel of John] had read Philo, it is difficult to imagine that the two were not part of the same Hellenistic Jewish tradition of interpretation and speculation."[25] In the Prologue, the author does not dwell on the details of language, but by failing to explain the concept of logos, he seems to assume that his readers are familiar with the concept.[26] As with Philo, John's use of the term *logos* includes an association with the creative aspects of divine language, "All things came to be through him" (John 1:3), and with the light associated with human reason. The claim that Jesus is the incarnation of the divine logos who "became flesh" (John 1:14) is clearly a step beyond traditional Jewish thought. The context of this claim is, however, entirely grounded in Philo's first-century Jewish understanding of the word of God mediated by human voices and language.

Philo's careful analysis of the properties of divine language as it was understood in the first century of the Common Era sheds light on several important aspects of the Christian experience of the word of God in the liturgical context. First, as Philo points out, divine language is unimaginably powerful. It is credited with the creation of human beings and their surrounding world. This creative capacity is linked to the ongoing power to transform human beings, giving them the capability to receive ongoing revelation. It takes the very shape of the logos, impressing the image of God on God's creation and making it possible for revelation to

25. Thomas Tobin, "The Prologue of John and Hellenistic Jewish Speculation," *Catholic Biblical Quarterly* 52 (1990): 262. See also David Runia, *Philo in Early Christian Literature: A Survey*, Jewish Traditions in Early Christian Literature (Minneapolis, MN: Fortress Press, 1993), 80–81.

26. Daniel Boyarin suggests that both Philo and John are drawing on a long tradition of Jewish midrash, which links *logos* theology with creation and salvation history. See Daniel Boyarin, "The Gospel of the *Memra:* Jewish Binitarianism and the Prologue to John," *Harvard Theological Review* 94, no. 3 (2001).

be processed and mediated to others. When the logos is experienced by human beings, it shapes their minds, just as a signet can mark a seal in melted wax. In the later Catholic Christian context, this permanently transformative power of the word of God is most often experienced in the sacramental rituals. As we will see below, Christian theologians such as Augustine also make use of the image of seal to emphasize the significance of the sacramental word in the transformation of Christians in baptism and Eucharist. Just as Philo understands the power of the logos to impress the image of God on creation, making it possible for them to receive divine revelation, so will later Christians attribute to the baptismal words the power of the spiritual seal which permanently marks the soul of a Christian.

Second, Philo is clear that the unmediated experience of divine language overwhelms human senses. This insight has clear implications for the sacraments. As Philo indicates, even the mediated experience of God's presence can be both frightening and confusing. Instead of hearing it, human beings might see, or feel, or taste, or smell it; even then it is too much for them to comprehend. Some sort of mediation is usually required. This could be a multisensory experience of the language of God or it could take the form of human language composed and recorded by other human beings in the Scriptures. Philo's foundational work on synesthesia and language indicates that both can be understood as transformative expressions of divine revelation mediated in "graspable units," which are suited to human understanding. Philo's approach to understanding the mediation of divine language is echoed in the multivalent signs of the Catholic liturgical tradition. In the sacraments we find not the direct, unmediated presence of God, but rather grace mediated through vision, taste, smell, and touch. This experience is not normally one of terrified confusion, but it nonetheless distributes the experience of God among the five senses.

Just as Philo is clear that the revelatory words of human language are not the literal, unprocessed words of God to humanity, so should members of the assembly remember that when the first lector ascends to the ambo at the Easter Vigil she is vocalizing the words of the sixth-century BCE Priestly writers who describe the orderly creation of the world by means of a language act of God. "In the beginning, when God created the heavens and the earth—and the earth was without form or shape, with darkness over the abyss and a mighty wind sweeping over the waters—Then God said: Let there be light, and there was light. God saw that the light was good. God then separated the light from the darkness. God called the light 'day,' and the darkness he called 'night.' Evening came, and morning followed—the first day" (Gen 1:1-5). It is not necessary, or even desirable, to claim that this poetic description is in fact the unmediated word of God spoken to the people. As Philo argues, the words of human poets mediating divine revelation also have the power to transform human beings. The work of the poet and the work of the lector are sacramental. Both offer their bodies and their voices as the medium for a divine presence which would otherwise be too overwhelming for the gathered assembly.

Writing in the same century in which Christianity originated, Philo provides an important foundation for subsequent Christian sacramental theology and theology of language. His work influenced both Ambrose and Augustine, whose theology grounds Western Christian sacramental theory. While frequently unacknowledged and in some cases outright disdained, Philo's theology of language not only provides context for the logos Christology of the Gospel of John but also sheds light on Augustine's fourth-century theology of language, which itself insists on the unity of word and sacrament.

Augustinian Foundations: Sacraments in the Context of Language

Augustine of Hippo's work on language, signs, and sacraments has become foundational for nearly all subsequent Western sacramental theology. Grounded both in a logos Christology and in his deep respect for the power and complexity of human language, Augustine attends to the relational and symbolic aspects of biblical revelation and the sacraments. He emphasizes that both require interpretation and that the ultimate check on any type of theological interpretation is to ask whether it results in the "twin love of God and neighbor."[27] We turn first to Augustine's understanding of language as a form of self-expression in relationship;

27. Augustine, *De doctrina Christiana*, trans. and ed. R. P. H. Green (New York: Clarendon Press, 1995), 1.36.40.

even human language has a power to transform because it mirrors the trinitarian, relational theology of God's self-expression. We will then examine the complexity of symbolic interpretation and the relationship that Augustine sees between the ways that symbols function in Scripture and sacrament.

A gifted bishop and rhetorician, Augustine was well aware of the great power that human language can wield. This power became especially clear to him in the experience of his own conversion, which was both mediated by several other human voices and was itself recorded in the written text of the *Confessions*.[28] In the eighth book of the *Confessions*, Augustine describes the prayer which immediately preceded his conversion experience. He begins his prayer by quoting Psalm 78, addressing his own plea to God in the voice of an ancient author. "And you, O Lord, how long? How long, O Lord, will you be angry forever? Remember not our past iniquities."[29] The response to his prayer comes in the form of the voice of a child chanting "Take up and read."[30] The child's voice sends him to yet another human author, this time Paul, in the form of the text of the Letter to the Romans. Finally Augustine turns to human conversation with his friend Alypius, who helps him to understand.[31] For Augustine, conversion is not an isolated experience that occurs only between himself and God. It is mediated by the words of his ancestors in faith, a child who is a stranger, and by a friend who helps him to interpret and understand. Augustine is also aware that he and other preachers and writers wield this power themselves when they address their audiences. As Edward Morgan points out, when the older Augustine reflects on what he has written in the *Confessions*, he observes that his own autobiographical writings have the power to "draw a person's mind and emotions towards [God]."[32] Augustine

28. See Edward Morgan, *The Incarnation of the Word: The Theology of Langauge of Augustine of Hippo* (London: T.&T. Clark, 2011), 23.

29. Augustine, "The Confessions," in *The Confessions of St. Augustine*, trans. and ed. John K. Ryan (New York: Doubleday, 1960), 8.12.28.

30. Ibid., 8.12.29.

31. Ibid., 8.12.30.

32. Augustine, *Revisions*, ed. John E. Rotelle, trans. Boniface Ramsey, The Works of Saint Augustine: A Translation for the 21st Century (New Rochelle, NY: New City Press, 2010), 2.6. See also Morgan, *The Incarnation of the Word*, 19.

does not claim that his writing was itself inspired by God in the way that the Scriptures are, but suggests that human language itself can mediate the offer of salvation in a variety of different ways. In his own experience, human words, spoken in the context of a variety of relationships, have mediated the presence of God and have transformed him.

Aware of the power that exists in language, Augustine is convinced that the human voice, in its written and spoken manifestations, is the privileged medium of God's self-communication because it echoes the patterns of the divine self-expression. As was the case with Philo, Augustine maintains a Platonic understanding of language, in which human language mirrors the logos, or word, of God. Suggesting a preexisting, ideal word which exists before speech, Augustine invites his reader to "understand how a word can be, not only before it is spoken aloud but even before the images of its sounds are turned over in thought."[33] Resituating the idea into a Christian context of logos Christology, Augustine observes that if one can imagine the possibility of a human word which exists before it is brought into speech, one can also then begin to understand "some likeness of that Word of which it is said, *In the beginning was the Word, and the Word was with God, and the Word was God* (John 1:1)."[34] For Augustine, the Word of God which existed from the beginning, before the creation of the world, the incarnation, or any other act of God's self-expression, presents a sacramental similarity between divine and human language. "An alignment takes place here between the concept of *verbum*, word, as the speech spoken by the human Christ, and *verbum* as the second

33. Augustine, *De Trinitate*, ed. John E. Rotelle, trans. Edmund Hill, The Works of Saint Augustine: A Translation for the 21st Century (New Rochelle, NY: New City Press, 1991), 2.15.19. See also *De doctrina Christiana*, in which Augustine connects the incarnation to human language. "It is something like when we talk; in order for what we have in mind to reach the minds of our hearers through their ears of flesh, the word which we have in our thoughts becomes a sound and is called speech. And yet this does not mean that our thought is turned into that sound, but while remaining undiminished in itself, it takes on the form of a spoken utterance by which to insert itself into their ears without bearing the stigma of any change in itself. That is how the Word of God was not changed in the least, and yet became flesh, in order to dwell among us." Augustine, *De doctrina Christiana*, 1.12.12.

34. Augustine, *De Trinitate*, 2.15.19.

person of the Trinity."[35] Augustine understands this incarnational alignment in sacramental terms. When Christ the Logos, speaks, "he speaks the Father's word, he speaks himself because he is the Father's Word."[36] As Morgan puts it, for Augustine, "it is through language's mediation that we can access the salvific effect of the Word's incarnation."[37] Here the words both signify and make present the reality of the trinitarian relationships; the verbal sign points to and actualizes the reality which it signifies.[38] In this sacramental Word, which is both proclaimed and enfleshed in the incarnation, "lies the salvation of all who believe, hope, and love."[39]

Augustine's understanding of human language is grounded in his Christology, which understands Christ as the Word of the Father. When human beings express themselves in human language, they both mirror the trinitarian relationships and continue to mediate God's plan of salvation. This can happen in everyday life, as Augustine's conversion experience demonstrates, but the process is also explicit in the Scriptures and in the sacramental rituals. In these contexts, Augustine attends carefully both to the divine and to the human characteristics of language. He is aware that in many cases the words of Scripture and sacrament function symbolically and must be interpreted, either through exegesis or mystagogy, so that they advance individuals and communities toward the "twin love of God and neighbor."[40] We turn first to Augustine's understanding of the way the words of Scripture function to transform and reveal. We will then turn to the sacramental rituals in which words also play key roles.

Augustine's approach to the language of Scripture emphasizes the sacramentality of the revelatory process. For Augustine, the Scriptures function efficaciously not because they are the unmediated words of God but

35. Morgan, *The Incarnation of the Word*, 134.

36. Augustine, *De Trinitate*, 1.26.

37. Morgan, *The Incarnation of the Word*, 53–54.

38. Drawing on the many parallels which exist between the figure of Lady Wisdom in the Wisdom literature and the figure of the *logos,* when Augustine discusses the way in which Wisdom is described as pouring forth from God in the Wisdom literature, he rejects any concern that "this means that it is not almighty itself, but only an outflow of the almighty . . . it was in order that the Word might become flesh." Augustine, *De Trinitate*, 4.27.

39. Ibid.

40. Augustine, *De doctrina Christiana*, 1.36.40.

rather because they are symbolic, transforming through the mediation of created realities. These created realities include the talents of the human authors, the processes of interpretation, and the symbolic images drawn from material reality.

Like Philo, Augustine makes no pretense that the Scriptures are the unmediated word of God. Rather, in the context of his awareness of the transformative power that human words derive from their analogous relationship to the divine self-communication, Augustine approaches Scriptural interpretation as a multifaceted conversation which takes place between God and humanity, and between human beings themselves. As Morgan notes, "[f]or Augustine we are never simply readers of the word. Instead, we are hearers of a canon of scriptural speakers with whom we may dynamically engage in the same way as we do with a disputant in a debate. . . . The words of the scriptural speaker and the speaker interpreting Scripture become the ground which we traverse as we engage with a greater dialogue with God."[41] It is in the context of this dialogue, which is structured on the deliberate choices that human beings make when speaking and writing, that Christians advance on the way to God and are in fact transformed within their social context by means of the words of other human speakers.[42]

This salvific transformation takes place in part through the metaphysical effect Augustine believes the words of Scripture can have on the human mind. Although his description differs somewhat from that of Philo, Augustine is aware of the transformative power of the Word of God active in the Scriptures as well as in the sacraments. As Rebecca Weaver describes it, for Augustine, "[e]ntrusting oneself to the language of [Scripture] not only teaches one what to desire but actually produces the desire in the one who is so taught."[43] Augustine himself discusses the ways in which Scripture can "give shape and form to human morals,"[44] molding

41. Morgan, *The Incarnation of the Word*, 94. Morgan makes reference to Augustine, *De doctrina Christiana*, 4.7.1.

42. As Morgan points out, this is true of Augustine's own conversion experience as discussed above.

43. Rebecca Weaver, "Prayer," in *Augustine through the Ages*, ed. Allan D. Fitzgerald (Grand Rapids, MI: Eerdmans, 1999), 672.

44. Augustine, *De doctrina Christiana*, 3.10.15.

readers or hearers into individuals who love God and neighbor appropriately. In a parallel to Philo's understanding of divine revelation as a kind of stamp or seal on the human intellect which then processes revelation for other human beings, Augustine's understanding of this transformative power of the Scriptures is grounded in the power of human language and in the work of the logos. In this way, it is comparable to the image of the sacramental seal which Augustine uses to describe the permanency of baptism.[45] Just as an individual can be shaped by the words of Scripture, so can she also be imprinted through the sacramental words spoken in the ritual, which, as we will see below, are also the words of the logos.

Given the complexities of human language as mediator for the word of God, Augustine is attentive to the problems that can occur when preachers and theologians seek to interpret the symbolic language of Scripture. In *De doctrina Christiana* he offers a clearly developed manual for biblical interpretation. It begins by insisting that "rules for dealing with the Scriptures"[46] are both necessary and helpful. Addressing people who believe that they can interpret the Scriptures without rules because they are the recipients of a "divine gift," Augustine reminds them that just as children learn to read and write and speak by "constantly hearing [their language] spoken,"[47] so must all Christians assimilate the rules for scriptural interpretation. Like any language, this one must be acquired through practice and through study with those who already know it. Augustine's rules include attention to the intentions of the human authors, including the various rhetorical devices the biblical authors may have used to make their points.[48]

As an example of Augustine's style of biblical interpretation, including its use of and differences from Philo, we turn to a case in which Augustine seeks to correct what he perceives to be a false interpretation that has led to heresy. In his interpretation of the description of Noah's ark, found in

45. Referring to baptism as "imprinted on [the individual] like a brand," Augustine insists that to rebaptize would be "to superimpose Christ on Christ." Augustine, "Exposition of Psalm 39," in *Expositions of the Psalms 33–50*, ed. John E. Rotelle, The Works of Saint Augustine: A Translation for the 21st Century (New Rochelle, NY: New City Press, 2000), 1.

46. Augustine, *De doctrina Christiana*, Preface, 1.

47. Ibid., Preface, 5.

48. Ibid., 3.37.38 and 3.29.40.

Genesis, Augustine agrees with Philo that words can point to multiple meanings, literal and allegorical.[49] Augustine faults Philo, however, for failing to grasp the sacramental dimension of the words of Scripture. For example, Augustine follows Philo for the interpretation of the ark as a symbol for the human body,[50] but relying on the work of Tyconius,[51] he adds that it should be more specifically understood as the body of Christ. Augustine then develops the image to suggest that the door of the ark points to the wound of Christ from which the sacraments, especially the Eucharist, flow.[52]

As Augustine's reinterpretation of the Philonic texts indicates, in the scriptural context, words function as types of signs which of themselves make "some other thing come to mind, besides the impression that [they] present . . . to the senses."[53] For Augustine, when the Scriptures are properly interpreted, they point to God's enduring transformative actions through texts, speech, and the created world. The incarnation itself is part of this tradition of sacramental mediation. If the ark is properly interpreted as the body of Christ, from whose sleeping side the sacraments pour forth, then, for Augustine, following in the interpretive footsteps of Ambrose, the ancient texts of Genesis can also prefigure the Christian

49. For a detailed comparison of these texts, see Runia, *Philo in Early Christian Literature: A Survey*, 322–23.

50. This text is contained in Philo's *Questions and Answers on Genesis*.

51. In this case, Augustine points out that Philo failed to apply Tyconius's rule pertaining to "the Lord and his body," which indicates that when "a text passes from head to body and from body to head, and yet still refers to one and the same person," the author intends to indicate not a human body, but rather Christ and the Church. Augustine, *De doctrina Christiana*, 3.31.44.

52. Referenced in *Sacrosanctum Concilium* 5, this powerful image can be found several times in Augustine's writings. As he writes in his Exposition on Psalm 40, "when did the Church's sacraments flow forth from Christ's side? While he slept on the cross." Augustine, "Exposition on Psalm 40," in *Expositions of the Psalms 33–50*, ed. John E. Rotelle, The Works of Saint Augustine: A Translation for the 21st Century (New Rochelle, NY: New City Press, 2000), 10. See also "Sermon 218.14," and "Expositions on the Psalms: 56.11, 102.10, 103[4].6, 126.7, 127.11, 138.2."

53. Augustine, *De doctrina Christiana*, 2.1.1. See also R. A. Markus, *Signs and Meanings: World and Text in Ancient Christianity* (Liverpool: Liverpool University Press, 1996), 87.

sacraments of baptism and Eucharist.[54] Far from innovative, the sacramental methods of saving humanity through material elements, such as water and wood, are deeply traditional. The waters around the ark prefigure the sacrament of baptism: "Noah, with his family is saved by water and wood, as the family of Christ is saved by baptism, as representing the suffering of the cross."[55] This water around the ark, like baptism, washes away sin and saves those who are safe within the boundaries of the church.[56]

This interpretive approach is in keeping with Augustine's broad understanding of the sacraments as signs that transform by pointing to spiritual realities beyond themselves.[57] Although he especially esteems the Christian ritual sacraments of baptism and Eucharist, Augustine also includes in the category of sacrament more general signs such as the rainbow, memorial celebrations such as Easter, the Lord's Prayer, circumcision, and dietary laws.[58] He rejects the idea that because the signs have changed,

54. As Hervé Savon notes, in the texts in which Ambrose borrows heavily from Philo or from other Alexandrian exegetes, he tends to steer his symbolic interpretation in the direction of baptism and Eucharist (Savon 325); Hervé Savon, *Saint Ambrose devant L'Exégèse de Philon le Juif* (Paris: Études Augustiniennes, 1977). "Ambrose replaces Philonic 'profane accessories,' where he finds them offensive o[r] superfluous, with the 'naked' words of scripture. Not only is the interpretation of scripture focused on Christ, but it is also redirected towards the liturgy of Christian worship, as embodied in baptism and the sacraments. It is a shift . . . from moral allegory to sacramental realism." Quoted in translation by David Runia. Runia, *Philo in Early Christian Literature: A Survey*, 304.

55. Augustine, *Answer to Faustus, a Manichean*, ed. Boniface Ramsey, The Works of St. Augustine: A Translation for the 21st Century (New Rochelle, NY: New City Press, 2007), 14.

56. Ibid., 16.20.

57. As Joanne McWilliam points out, Augustine's *Answer to Faustus* marks a shift in his sacramental theology. Prior to this point, Augustine had tended to think of sacraments as kinds of signs. By the year 399, however, " 'sign' had changed from representing sensible objects to encompassing spiritual realities past and present, as well." Joanne McWilliam, "Weaving the Strands Together: A Decade in Augustine's Eucharistic Theology," in *Collectanea Augustiniana*, ed. Mathijs Lamberigts, Bernard Bruning, and J. van Houtem (Louvain: Leuven University Press, 1990), 497–98.

58. Elsewhere he notes that "there is a sacrament in a celebration when the commemoration of the event is carried out in such a way that it is understood also to

"the realities themselves are also different which the prophetic religion foretold as promised and which the gospel religion has announced as fulfilled."[59] Emphasizing that just as people may describe a reality in different ways, God may use different sacraments to announce the same spiritual realities, Augustine establishes a clear connection between the signs included in the Old Testament and the sacramental signs practiced by Christians. In both cases, whether in mystagogical preaching to the newly baptized, or in exegetical work on ancient texts, signs must be properly interpreted so that they "make some other thing come to mind, besides the impression that [they] present . . . to the senses."[60]

For Augustine, signs are found both in the natural world and in the world of texts and communication. They are a central aspect of his theology of language, since words are the primary example of a sign functioning as it ought. "Words, after all, are far and away the principal means used by human beings to signify the thoughts they have in their minds whenever anyone wishes to express them."[61] A word is something that is perceived by the eyes or by the ears and that is not only a sound or a sight but also something that brings something else to mind. This process of signification occurs when one reads the Scriptures, hears a sermon, experiences the sacraments, or simply converses with someone else.

In the context of the sacraments, which Augustine refers to as "visible words,"[62] the words and the elements function together both to teach and to transform individuals and communities. The material elements of bread, wine, and water are visible signs which point to something beyond themselves.[63] The sacramental words, however, also function as

---

signify something that must be received in a Holy manner." Augustine, "Letter 55: Augustine to Januarius," in *Letters 1-99*, The Works of Saint Augustine: A Translation for the 21st Century, ed. John E. Rotelle (Brooklyn: New City Press, 2001). See also Augustine, *Answer to Faustus, a Manichean*, 19.16.

59. Augustine, *Answer to Faustus, A Manichean*, 19.16.

60. Augustine, *De doctrina Christiana*, 2.1.1.

61. Augustine, *De doctrina Christiana*, 2.3.4.

62. Augustine, *Answer to Faustus, A Manichean*, 19.16, and Augustine, *Tractates on the Gospel of John, 55–111*, ed. Thomas P. Halton, trans. John W. Rettig, The Fathers of the Church (Washington, DC: CUA Press, 1994), 80.3.

63. Augustine observes that most people find it more pleasant to learn with visual aids. Augustine, *De doctrina Christiana*, 2.6.8.

signs which point beyond themselves to invisible spiritual realities. Playing on the link between human language and the incarnation, Augustine emphasizes the role of the spoken word as sacramental sign. He observes that "this bread and wine, when the word is applied to it, becomes the body and blood of the Word."[64] The process by which such words and signs operate mirrors the divine process by which the divine word is offered to humanity. The significance of this sacramental word becomes still clearer in Augustine's dispute with the Donatists about the validity of baptism. Addressing the question of whether or not a person is baptized if the baptizing minister is in a state of schism, Augustine is clear that the true minister of the sacrament is Christ. The state of the minister is not of grave consequence because when a person is baptized "[t]he seed of which [she is] born again is the Word of God."[65] In the sacraments, the verbal signs of human language point to the spiritual reality of God's self-expression offered to the individual in the baptismal rite. The created realities of human voices, water, and ritual actions are perceived by the senses and point to the spiritual reality of baptism. Here "language" can be said to apply not only to the spoken words but also to the material signs and ritual actions that function together with the words to convey meaning.

Augustine's theology of language offers several helpful insights into the reality of the unity of word and sacrament. First, given Augustine's background as a teacher of rhetoric, as well as his day-to-day ministry of preaching, writing, and celebrating the sacraments, his appreciation for the power of human language is clear. This is in part due to its analogous relationship with the word of God. Because it is so powerful in its own right, language is able to carry the weight of mediating God's revelation offered to humanity,

64. Augustine, "Sermon 229: On Holy Easter Sunday about the Sacraments of the Faithful," in *Sermons on the Liturgical Seasons (184-229Z).* The Works of Saint Augustine: A Translation for the 21st Century, ed. John E. Rotelle (New Rochelle, NY: New City Press, 1993), 1. Augustine makes the same point regarding baptism in a commentary on the Gospel of John. See Augustine, *Tractates on the Gospel of John, 55–111*, 80.3.

65. Augustine, "In Answer to the Letters of Petilian, the Donatist," in *Augustin: The Writings Against the Manicheans and Against the Donatists*, ed. Peter Schaff, Nicene and Post-Nicene Fathers of the Church (Peabody, MA: Hendrickson, 1995), 7.8.

fundamentally in Scripture and sacramental rituals, but also in human conversation, other spiritual books, and signs that are not ritual sacraments. Augustine's theology of language lays the groundwork for thinking about language sacramentally as a created reality capable of mediating the presence of God. When Scripture and sacraments are considered in the broader context of language events, their similarities become clearer.

Second, for Augustine, "language" indicates the process by which a speaker shares signs of the reality of who he or she is. When a person shares her thoughts through words or gestures, or when God reveals Godself in Christ the Word, a relationship is established by means of signs. Augustine points out that words are especially good examples of what a sign does, but no one expects a person to speak without using visual cues such as gestures or facial expressions, or to write without references to images that can both engage the reader and illustrate a point. For Augustine, God does the same, sometimes using only words, other times using symbols such as the ark or bread and wine to effect revelation in a manner that engages several of the senses. In the cases in which visual symbols or symbols which engage the other senses are used, word and element are not separate items but function together as a composite symbol or "visible word" expressing the single reality. Augustine's understanding of language can help us to see that words and symbols operate together for the same purposes. There is thus no tension between the proclamation of Scripture, which includes symbols, or the consecration of the Eucharist, which relies on the word of Christ.

Since Scripture and sacraments are both language events, each requires interpretation. It is unrealistic to think that one will be clearer than the other, simply because one is comprised primarily of words or because the other includes material symbols that engage the human senses of taste, smell, and vision. The signs of Scripture and sacrament point to spiritual realities beyond themselves. The person who takes them only at face value may find herself worshipping food items or thinking of the Bible as the result of voice-dictation software. For Augustine, the many levels of meaning found in the text reflect the authorial intentions of the human beings who wrote, as well as the divine revelation human beings can begin to experience when they interpret the Scriptures correctly.

Finally, rooted in his understanding of the power of human language and the connection between human speech and the incarnation of the logos, Augustine recognizes the transformative potential of both the Scriptures and the sacraments. Like Philo, he is aware that encounters with the Scriptures can have transformative effects. This is true in the case of his own conversion experience and is also true more broadly in the sense that reading the Scriptures can shape an individual into a more moral person. He thus builds on Philo and advances the conversation with his theology of sacraments grounded in a theology of language. As is the case in scriptural experiences of transformative revelation, Augustine's sacramental theology also emphasizes the permanent effects of the word of God. The mark of baptism is "imprinted" on those who are baptized. The celebration of the Eucharist transforms the assembly into the very body and blood of Christ which they celebrate. "What you receive is what you yourselves are . . . what you see here is the sacrament of unity."[66] Because these are the actions of the very Word of God, they cannot be reversed. The Word which brought the world into being continues to transform and recreate through human language events.

Experiencing the Word of God in a Postmodern Context

In the first verses of Genesis, the idea of a God who creates and relates through language is established as foundational for the Judeo-Christian tradition. In our own time, the questions surrounding divine and human language are no less urgent. Tensions exist between Christians who claim that the Bible is the literal word of God and those who emphasize its historical context, those who wait for the sacramental words of institution and those who are sustained by the preached word of the homily. In the mid-twentieth century, Karl Rahner laid the foundations for a twenty-first-century understanding of the unity of word and sacrament under the aegis of language. Emphasizing the fundamental unity of God's word offered to humanity at various times and places in history, Rahner argued explicitly for a theological understanding of the unity of word and sacrament. Postmodern theologians such as Louis-Marie Chauvet and

66. Augustine. "Sermon 229A: On Holy Easter Sunday about the Sacraments of the Faithful," in *Sermons on the Liturgical Seasons (184-229Z)*, The Works of Saint Augustine: A Translation for the 21st Century, ed. John E. Rotelle (New Rochelle, NY: New City Press, 1993), 1.

Jean-Luc Marion subsequently developed theologies of language which highlighted the role of difference in communication and the excess of meaning which is found in symbols such as the word of God. We turn first to Rahner's foundational work and then to the postmodern insights that continue to shape contemporary theologies of language.

Karl Rahner's contributions to a theological understanding of the unity of word and sacrament are grounded in the theological-anthropological claim that human beings are created as "hearers of the word," whose lifelong vocation is to respond with faith to God's divine self-communication.[67] For Rahner, when human beings listen for God's word offered to them in history, they must remember that they are waiting not for a series of pronouncements or even commandments, but rather for the singular and simple word of God. "God does not say all sorts of things to men, and his words are not a miscellany of disconnected subjects. In the last resort he utters only one thing, which is himself as eternal salvation in the Spirit of the incarnate Logos of God."[68] It is the experience or encounter with this divine utterance which is salvific for humanity. Humans live out their vocations by waiting with hope for God's self-revelation. They experience salvation when they encounter the "one thing alone, which belongs to God's own reality: the word that sets the creature free from its muteness by pointing beyond the whole created order."[69] This word is the reality of the presence of God.[70] When they recognize their own finitude in the face of this mysterious word, which human beings are uniquely equipped to

67. See for example, Karl Rahner, *Hearer of the Word: Laying the Foundation for a Philosophy of Religion*, ed. Andrew Tallon, trans. Joseph Donceel (New York: Continuum, 1994); and Karl Rahner, *Foundations of Christian Faith: An Introduction to the Idea of Christianity*, trans. William V. Dych (New York: Crossroad, 1997), 24–43.

68. Karl Rahner, "The Word and the Eucharist," in *Theological Investigations 4* (New York: Crossroad, 1982), 278.

69. Karl Rahner, "Priest and Poet," in *Theological Investigations 3* (New York: Crossroad, 1982), 303.

70. To speak of the word of God "means that the grace of God is not merely spoken of but takes place as an event in this utterance." Rahner, "The Word and the Eucharist," 263.

receive, Christians become aware of God's presence beyond the created order and address themselves back to God in faith and worship.[71]

Rahner follows Augustine's pattern of understanding the word of God as the transformative expression of who God is in relationship, mediated by human language. Because human beings are spiritual yet historically grounded beings, "the supernatural reality can display itself only through the medium of the human *word*."[72] In agreement with both Philo and Augustine, Rahner believes that human language is an especially apt medium for divine self-communication. As Sandra Schneiders would later put it, encounter with God through the word allows "for the mutual gift of selves."[73] Language is the medium for relationships. For Rahner and for other theologians of the twentieth century, the phrase "word of God" refers not only, or even primarily, to revealed information. It is, rather, the revelation of the possibility and reality of relationship.

Divine revelation thus shares many characteristics with human language. It can occur not only through spoken words but also through various types of signs, symbols, and gestures. The effects of the divine word are simply more intense experiences of the ways in which human language already functions. Rahner points to the "primordial words"[74] of the poet, which both express and evoke the deepest meaning of what it means to be human. He emphasizes that human words, far from ephemeral, can have lasting implications for the individuals and communities who hear them. "A word in its *human* reality is not completely dependent on and just merely coexistent to its sound in the physical world. A word of love, a promise, a threat still exist after their audible expression has passed away."[75] The inherent strength of human language mediates the divine encounter. The divine word does not break the structure of human

71. John M. McDermott, "The Christologies of Karl Rahner," *Gregorianum* 67 (1986): 113.

72. Rahner, "The Word and the Eucharist," 267. See also Rahner, *Hearer of the Word*, 134.

73. Sandra M. Schneiders, *The Revelatory Text: Interpreting the New Testament as Sacred Scripture*, 2nd ed. (Collegeville, MN: Liturgical Press, 1999), 35.

74. Rahner, "Priest and Poet," 296.

75. Rahner, "The Word and the Eucharist," 262.

language, but works within it, building on it in ways that deliberately blur the boundaries between nature and grace.[76]

Even as it builds on human language, the divine word comes to human beings in the natural mediations of their voices, their books, their communities, their gestures and their celebrations. While Rahner is clear that the word of God may be heard in any time and place in history, he privileges the ecclesial context in which the word of God may be heard publicly and consciously. He argues, for instance, that it is in the sacraments that Christians experience "the most intensive instance of God's revealing word insofar as it is addressed to individuals in a peak moment of their life of faith, by the proper and ultimate messenger of this revealed word, that is, by the Church."[77] Rahner's understanding of the church as the most appropriate messenger for the Word of God is rooted in his christological ecclesiology. This approach first considers the logos as the symbol which allows the reality of who God is to be present in history.[78] It then regards the church as the public symbol which makes it possible for the logos to be present in every historical time and place.[79] The symbol of the church is not the same thing as the reality of God, yet the actions of the church function as signs or landmarks that point to God's presence in the history

76. As Rahner says in his essay "Nature and Grace," "Our actual nature is *never* 'pure' nature. It is a nature installed in a supernatural order which man can never leave, even as a sinner and unbeliever. . . . [One who is aware from revelation of the order of grace] must allow for the fact that much of his concrete experience which he is almost automatically tempted to attribute to his 'nature' may perhaps in fact be the effect in him of what he must recognize as unmerited grace in the light of theology." Karl Rahner, "Nature and Grace," in *Theological Investigations 4*, 183.

77. Karl Rahner, "Faith and Sacrament," in *Theological Investigations 23* (New York: Crossroad, 1983), 183. See also: Rahner, "Priest and Poet," 306.

78. As Rahner puts it, "the Logos, as Son of the Father, is truly, in his humanity as such, the revelatory symbol in which the Father enunciates himself, in this Son, to the world—revelatory because the symbol renders present what has been revealed." Rahner, "The Theology of the Symbol," in *Theological Investigations 4*, 239.

79. "When we say that the Church is the persisting presence of the incarnate Word in space and time, we imply at once that it continues the symbolic function of the Logos in the world." Ibid., 240.

of the world.[80] The ecclesial context, and especially the liturgy, is thus the most appropriate and significant venue for the divine-human encounter mediated by human language. This liturgical encounter is comprised of various elements including the human words of praise offered to God, the proclamation of the scriptural word of God, and the celebration of the sacraments in which words, gestures, and material elements function together to signify the transformative presence of God.

In contrast to the prevailing Catholic theology of his time, which emphasized the sacraments to the detriment of the proclaimed word, Rahner sought to consider the two as a united whole. He writes, "there can be no question of dividing up and distributing the effects . . . as between word and sacrament."[81] Since there is really only one Word of God spoken to humanity, word and sacrament are "phases and moments of the same process . . . each phase shares the being of the whole, the *whole* reality is truly present and effective in each phase."[82] Here it is the phases that function as symbols to mediate the undivided presence of God. One cannot distribute grace, but only recognize it, as Rahner does, as "present always and everywhere from beginning to end, from the first word of preaching to the sacrament inclusively, in the form of the word."[83] The proclamation and preaching of Scripture, as well as the sacramental rituals, are thus best understood as more narrow instances within the broader category of the word of God offered to humanity in history.

While some instances of the word may be more efficacious than others, the divine self-offer cannot be reduced to any single part of the liturgy, or even to the liturgy itself.[84] As with human communication, the most efficacious or significant words must be understood in the larger context of a

80. Karl Rahner, "What Is a Sacrament?," in *Theological Investigations 14* (New York: Crossroad, 1983), 137–38.

81. Rahner, "The Word and the Eucharist," 286.

82. Ibid., 279.

83. Ibid., 286. See also "What Is a Sacrament?," 137, where Rahner suggests that a theology of the word "could perfectly well become the basis for a theology of the sacraments."

84. "Each word of God in the Church takes on, in keeping with its significance within the whole, the character—analogously and in a lower degree—of the one whole word of God." Rahner, "The Word and the Eucharist," 279. See also Rahner, "Priest and Poet," 296–98.

relationship, and the sacraments are best "understood as one quite specific word-event within a theology of the word."[85] Rahner finds this perspective to be ecumenically helpful in moving toward unity around the relationship between word and sacrament. He also believes that reference to the Eucharist as "a sacramental 'word' event"[86] has the effect of orienting the recipient of the sacrament away from his or her own personal concerns and toward "the proclamation of the presence of the Lord's death as bringing about salvation [which] takes place within the community as such and for it as such."[87] Since language is inherently relational; when one considers the sacraments in this context, concerns for other Christians and for the larger human community become more evident.

Rahner's theology of language was foundational for the twentieth century and for subsequent Catholic sacramental theology. His insights into the relational implications of divine revelation and his attention to the sacraments as moments within a larger theology of the word have laid the groundwork for later theologians to consider sacramental theology from the perspective of theology of language. Among these postmodern theologians, Louis-Marie Chauvet has been among the most influential for recontextualizing sacramental theology in this framework.

As discussed above, the relationship in difference between the divine word and the human words which often express it is a complicated one. While ancient authors such as Philo tended to think of language and the senses as things which are deployed to express or retrieve information conveyed to the mind, postmodern theologians such as Chauvet would insist that language must be understood as a *context* in which human beings experience their relationships with one another and with the divine Other. This language context is not something constructed by human beings, but rather is given to them by God. Individuals are born into language and operate within it to develop their own identities and relationships with other human beings and with God.

To speak of the words of the Bible or the content of divine revelation as "the word of God" is thus to imply a point of unitive encounter within difference between God's creative communication and the communication

85. Rahner, "What Is a Sacrament?," 138.

86. Ibid., 141.

87. Ibid.

which takes place between human beings. The phrase "the word of God" can be understood as a metaphor, a term which indicates a necessary poetic tension between like and unlike.[88] The phrase "word of God" thus does not imply literal divine speech, but rather language which facilitates relationship. To say that God speaks a word to humanity captures the human intuition that God wishes a relationship with us and that we in some way are equipped to receive this communication. As postmodern theologian Jean-Luc Marion describes it, the divine word "saturates" all human words or signs that seek to express it; the divine word overflows humanity's preconceived boundaries of language and communication. It builds on the relationship structures of human beings, but exceeds them, confusing the senses and complicating the relationships.[89] As Chauvet points out, the *difference* between God and humanity is what makes this type of communication possible. This is not a difference of separation, but rather a "*difference* . . . intrinsically connected to an *identity* or likeness between two realities."[90] It is in the language act that identity and difference become most clear and that human beings recognize both the distinctions and the relationships that exist between themselves and the Other. In this moment, they are both united with God and most aware of themselves as different in relationship.

In our own time, Christians may find themselves asking the either/or questions: divine word or human word? Scripture or sacrament? Contemporary theology invites us to think of these differences not as points of separation but as places of *likeness* in relationship. From the work of late twentieth- and early twenty-first-century theologians, we are invited to think about language more broadly. First, language is presented not as a tool but rather as a context. This shift in perspective has implications for considering the ways language works both for us and on us. Second,

88. See for example, Sandra M. Schneiders, *Women and the Word: The Gender of God in the New Testament and the Spirituality of Women* (New York: Paulist Press, 1986), 25.

89. Jean-Luc Marion, *God without Being: Hors-texte*, trans. Thomas A. Carlson (Chicago: University of Chicago Press, 1991), 156.

90. Louis-Marie Chauvet, *Symbol and Sacrament: A Sacramental Reinterpretation of Christian Existence*, trans. Patrick Madigan and Madeleine Beaumont (Collegeville, MN: Liturgical Press, 1995), 503.

when we consider language as a system of communication, it becomes clear that it is not only information which is conveyed but also our very selves in relationship with one another and in relationship with God.

The concept of language as context is most fully developed in Chauvet's work but is also hinted at in Rahner's understanding of a liturgy of the world,[91] which provides the context for the liturgy of the church. To consider language as the context for all that we do reminds us that words and symbols are not items created and dispatched by a single individual for a single purpose. Words and symbols preexist every individual and thus transform us into social beings, even as we learn their uses and effects. As we develop within this language context, human beings come to realize that language itself is transformative. It shapes both our thought-options (it is difficult to think of something if no word exists to describe it) and our relationships. As Rahner points out, powerful words (or gestures) of love or hate make lasting impressions on who we are. Emotions which are evoked or expressed by language leave us transformed as beings who know that we are loved, or perhaps conversely, bereft. An understanding of language as a preexisting context for human life and experience helps to illustrate the power of human language. When God "speaks" to human beings in this context, God makes use of this existing power. Grace builds on nature to effect spiritual transformation according to the same systems that human beings use to effect emotional transformation. In both cases, the transformation is powerful and lasting.

As Rahner points out, God speaks only one word to humanity and that word is not merely informational but is God's very self. Recent theologies of language illuminate the relational capacities of words, spoken and written, as well as gestures and other signs. When the depths of feeling are conveyed, spoken words are often accompanied by gestures. A declaration of love is most fully represented by both words and gestures (a kiss or an embrace). In this case, that which is indicated overflows the capacity of isolated words. In the context of the divine human relationship, we must expect that God's very presence may overflow the capacity of any one element of language. In this case, the sacramental unity of word and element can sometimes best convey the presence of God in words and gestures. The divine presence in the reading of the Scriptures and in the

91. This phrase will be discussed in greater detail in chapter 4.

sacramental word and sacramental element are the same presence, but operate together to more adequately express that which is beyond our understanding. The divine presence can no more be divided than the gesture of love can be separated from the words of love.

Conclusion

When the lector ascends to the ambo to read the first chapter of Genesis at the Easter Vigil, she is mediating words that would have been familiar to Philo and Augustine. The twenty-first-century lector might be reading the familiar words in English, or Spanish, or Tagalog, or Haitian Creole. Perhaps she is aware of the documentary hypothesis that suggests a sixth-century BCE priestly source. Perhaps she is struck by the repetition of phrases or the poetic order of the text. When she looks out into the assembly, she may seek the eyes of a family member for encouragement or the eyes of a stranger in welcome. She might be aware as she stands and proclaims the creation narrative rooted in the creative word of God, that down the street, and in the next state, and around the world, Easter fires are being lit and assemblies are settling in to keep vigil, to hear the ancestral stories, to celebrate the ancient rites, and to try to articulate the central Christian mysteries through candles and flowers, words, colors, song and posture, the touching of hands in the sign of peace, the flick of Easter water cast from the aisle, the food that is offered, the drink that is sipped, incense which clouds and scents the air, and human bodies, dressed in their very best, crowded into hard pews and awaiting the word which proclaims and makes present the resurrection.

This word, proclaimed in human language by the voice of the lector, the voice of the priest, and in the many symbols that fill the sanctuary, cannot be neatly divided into a "biblical word" or a "sacramental word." It is the one word, spoken in many human languages and revealing who God is to the gathered assembly. The lens of language offers us new insights into the Liturgy of the Word and the Liturgy of the Eucharist, while also pointing toward their inherent unity.

As the lens of language illustrates, spoken and written words serve as mediators of reality. Words are not somehow more pure than symbols merely because, in their spoken form, they lack materiality. While this gnostic tendency can be found throughout the history of Christianity, a careful look at the tradition clearly demonstrates the ways in which words act as mediators of revelation. Both Philo and Augustine recognized the mediated aspect of Scripture. Not the "pure" unmediated word of God, these texts, inscribed on scrolls and codices, offer the word of God as it has been mediated through the human author, writing in his or her own time and place. This author is not merely a passive conduit, but is a true mediator, whose actions allow the divine word to be heard and understood by other human beings. In this way, the Scriptures stand at the intersection of the relationship between God and human beings and between human beings and their ancestors in faith. When we hear the words of Scripture proclaimed in the liturgy, we are invited to be aware of the individuals and groups who offered themselves as mediators. We are invited to remember the copyists, bookbinders, editors, translators, and scholars whose work mediates the word of God in any given time and place. As Augustine pointed out, no one expects a speaker to speak with only his or her tongue. Expressions, gestures, and other symbolic movements convey meaning in a manner inseparable from the words spoken. The words of language cannot be isolated from the embodied humans who make them visible and audible to the rest of humanity. This realization leads us to a deeper appreciation of the incarnation itself as the highest form of sacramental mediation for the Word of God.

The lens of language also contributes to a deeper understanding of the sacraments. As early as Augustine, sacraments have been described as "visible words"; yet for many Catholics, the sacramental focus tends to be on the material element, at times to the exclusion of the words. Such habits, fostered in the medieval and Tridentine practices of silent eucharistic prayers and elaborate ritual elements for the showing of the consecrated host, resulted in an overemphasis on the "matter" of the sacrament, rather than on the ritual words. The perspective of language can provide a corrective to this balance, demonstrating that the sacrament may be understood to be effective due to the transformative power of language. This transformative potential of language must be understood in two ways. As Karl Rahner points out, human language can itself be transformative of persons and relationships, even when it takes place only between human beings. Philo's understanding of the logos of God indicates that the transformative nature of human language is due to its connection with the divine self-expression. Language and reason are ways in which human beings participate in traits that originate with God. In the sacraments, the word of God is mediated by the words, symbols, and gestures of human beings. Since revelation always overflows or "saturates" the human capacity to express it, the sacraments rely on words, gestures, and symbols (all of which are elements of language) to begin to convey the transformative reality of God's salvific presence in the community.

These deeper understandings of scriptural proclamation and sacramental celebration indicate the fundamental unity of word and sacrament. When viewed through the lens of language, it becomes clear that the Liturgy of the Word and the Liturgy of the Eucharist are instances of human language, broadly construed, being used to mediate God's revelatory presence. Both offer the possibility of communication and the development of a transformative relationship between divine and human. This relationship is rooted in God's initiative to communicate with human beings through the Logos, incarnate in Jesus of Nazareth, and existing as the self-communication of God from the beginning. Given the *difference* between God and humanity, the divine encounter, in word and sacrament, must always be understood as transformative. While Catholics are quick to recognize the permanence of a spiritual change effected by the sacraments of baptism, ordination, or marriage, the ancient connections to the transformative nature of an encounter with other forms of the word of God are sometimes forgotten. As Philo and Augustine make clear, these divine encounters, often experienced both aurally and visually, also leave their spiritual mark on humanity. These spiritual transformations, or "imprints" on the mind or soul, are not only, or perhaps even primarily, for the sake of the individual. The transformative encounter with God is what makes it possible for God's revelation to be conveyed to humanity in enduring textual form. Likewise, the transformative encounters in the sacraments strengthen individuals to act as leaders in society, in their families, and in their church communities.

chapter 4

The Sacramentality of the Liturgy

A Holy and Vulnerable Unity

Several semesters ago, one of my students gave an excellent presentation on the Roman Canon. She clearly explained the themes of sacrifice and offering, the communion of saints, and the words of institution in this particular eucharistic prayer. Stumbling slightly over the recent translation of the third edition of the Roman Missal, however, she also repeatedly referred to the "holy and vulnerable" hands of Jesus which handled the chalice and the bread. Although unintentional, her careful repetition of "holy and vulnerable," rather than "holy and *venerable*" as the translation would have it, points to the heart of the Catholic understanding of sacramentality. Hands can be holy not only when they are "venerable" but also when they are "vulnerable." As Jesus approached the Last Supper, his hands were perhaps more overtly vulnerable than venerable. Within hours they would be pierced and bleeding. Vulnerable indeed, but no less holy.

The term sacramentality refers to the conviction that all material reality has the potential to mediate the presence of God.[1] As a framework for considering the inherent unity of the liturgy, the concept of sacramentality

1. See for example, Richard P. McBrien, "Sacramentality, principle of," in *The HarperCollins Encyclopedia of Catholicism*, ed. Richard P. McBrien (San Francisco: HarperCollins, 1995).

encourages Christians to consider the graced nature of the world and the unity of all creation as mediator of the presence of God. This perspective, present in the magisterial theology of Thomas Aquinas, as well as in the biblical sources of the Wisdom literature, was retrieved in the twentieth century as a context for understanding the sacraments. More recently, it has also been suggested as a most appropriate context for considering the transformative nature of the word of God. When viewed through the lens of sacramentality, the "one table of word of God and Body of Christ" (DV 21) is revealed as a gift which emerges from the context of graced creation. The human beings who are nourished at this table experience themselves as graced but limited, cared for by God, yet destined and able to contribute to the ongoing sacramentality of the world.

To consider the unity of the liturgy in the context of the sacramentality of the world, we turn first to the work of Thomas Aquinas on the relationship between nature and grace. Aquinas's conviction that grace and nature are always experienced as intertwined, and that "grace does not scrap nature but brings it to perfection,"[2] is at the heart of the Catholic understanding of sacramentality. This conviction reflects the earlier biblical understanding of the created world as essentially good, even in its natural state, because it is made and sustained with Wisdom by God. Despite human sinfulness the world is not abandoned by God, but is accompanied by the same divine Wisdom which shaped the world and continues to sustain it through God's presence in word and sacrament. The chapter will conclude with the recontextualization of language and sacramental rituals under the category of sacramentality. This retrieval and recontextualization sheds new light on the unity of word and sacrament as well as on a twenty-first-century understanding of the unity of the liturgy.

A Thomistic Understanding of Nature and Grace

Aquinas begins his *Summa Theologiae* with a discussion of the natural world—a description of the world as it was created by God, with strengths and, as my student put it, vulnerabilities. The world is described as it would be without any kind of supernatural assistance from God. According to

2. Thomas Aquinas, *Summa Theologiae* (New York: Blackfriars and McGraw-Hill, 1963), I, q. 1, a. 8, ad. 2.

this understanding of creation, every creature has a natural capacity for certain kinds of excellence. These degrees of excellence require God's initiative to begin, but can be maintained without ongoing assistance from God; they should be valued as part of the inherent goodness of the created world. Aquinas begins with this description in order to set up a discussion of the relationship between God and the created world in history. As Aquinas understands it, God respects the integrity of creation, and could allow it to proceed without the accompaniment of grace. This, however, is not the Christian experience in history. Drawing from Scripture, tradition, and reason, Aquinas argues that in addition to respecting the goodness of creation, God sometimes provides supernatural help which works in tandem with nature to allow creatures to exceed their natural limitations. Aquinas's conviction that nature and supernatural assistance (grace) are never in conflict with one another, but rather work together, provides a foundation for the Catholic understanding of sacramentality.

To illustrate this point, we will consider two examples from the category of created nature. For Aquinas, the nature of any kind of being is reflective of the power that God has given "for efficacy in respect of some definite actualization to which it can proceed in accordance with the nature proper to it."[3] Thus, any creature's nature consists of the powers which it is given by God, at its creation, in order to act. As an example, Joseph Wawrykow contrasts the nature of a squirrel to the nature of a human being. By her nature, a human person has the capacity to "think discursively and to will . . . to know whatever presents itself to the senses."[4] Thinking, willing, and knowing through sensory perception are thus qualities which are natural to human beings. Neither good nor evil in themselves, they are simply qualities which can be attributed to the type of being known as human. "In contrast," Wawrykow adds, "the squirrel lacks the capacity to think and will . . . it simply senses and acts on instinct. If . . . one were to ask the squirrel to follow, perhaps even contribute to, an argument, that would be to ask of the squirrel what lies beyond its natural capacity."[5] The

3. Ibid., I-II, q. 109, a. 1.

4. Joseph Wawrykow, "Grace," in *The Theology of Thomas Aquinas*, ed. Rik Van Nieuwenhove and Joseph Wawrykow (Notre Dame, IN: University of Notre Dame Press, 2005), 193.

5. Ibid., 193.

fact that the squirrel cannot act beyond its natural capacity is a limitation, but not a reflection of evil in the squirrel. The squirrel has the capacity to achieve excellence according to its nature. This excellence does not take the form of thinking, willing, or discoursing, but it does manifest itself in sensing, acting on instinct, and running vertically up trees. Humans cannot run vertically up trees because it is not in their nature to do so. Thus human capacity is naturally limited as well, but the excellence that both human beings and squirrels can attain, each according to their natures, is regarded as fundamentally good. As Elizabeth Johnson puts it,

> In this framework, creatures . . . exist with their own integrity and are themselves properly agents and causes, in participated finite ways, with a difference from God that is ultimately and essentially good. We encounter that goodness not merely in looking past creatures to their Source, but also in looking at them, in celebrating their intrinsic density and their irreplaceable uniqueness. At the same time, they exist because the loving Giver of life shares the plenitude of being as the grounding source of their existence at every moment.[6]

As Johnson makes clear, creation exists only because of God and is called to participation with God. These relationships, however, do not detract from the goodness of each creature, which achieves excellence according to its nature.

Working from this foundation, Aquinas makes the further point that, human beings can be created with natures orienting them toward something beyond their natural abilities. For example, just as squirrels do not have the natural capacity to think, will, or discourse, neither do human beings have the natural capacity to achieve the end of union with God, which God intends for them. Although this higher end is by no means attainable through human nature alone, the orientation toward the higher end (requiring the intervention of God) is included in that which may be considered natural to the human.[7] In their created state of perfection

6. Elizabeth A. Johnson, *Ask the Beasts: Darwin and the God of Love* (New York: Bloomsbury, 2014), 148.

7. "[H]uman nature, by the very fact that it is of a nobler kind, can be led to some higher end, at least by the assistance of grace." Aquinas, *Summa Theologiae*, I-II, q. 109, a. 5, ad. 3.

before the Fall, humans could, by "natural endowments . . . will and perform the good which was proportionate to [their] own nature."[8] This goodness extended to the natural act of loving God above all things. In this state of integrity, before the Fall, a human being in the state of perfect human nature could, once initially moved by God, love God above all things because it is the natural and rational thing to do.[9] She would thus be oriented toward union with God, although unable to achieve this unity on her own efforts. Because the natural state of human beings is the result of God's creation, it is itself good, although ultimately insufficient for humans to achieve their final, supernatural, end with God. To achieve this end, grace is required to heal the soul of original sin and illuminate the mind regarding matters of supernatural revelation.

Since the supernatural end with God, desired by human beings and by God, is beyond the natural capacity of humanity, the possibility of union with God can be the result only of the gift of grace from God. Aquinas understands grace either as God's very presence (uncreated grace) or, as Stephen Duffy puts it, as a "created gift superadded to natural human powers."[10] In this case, something is added to the natural capacities of human beings, allowing them to achieve that which is fundamentally beyond their created abilities. Such an addition can be regarded as only the generous gift of God. While it is possible to imagine a hypothetical "natural" state in which humans might exist without grace, in human lived reality, the presence of grace is a constant. For Aquinas, the nature of every created thing, while limited, is itself good; it is created by God out of God's loving goodness and thus has the capacity to reflect the goodness of the Creator. In the reality of human lived experience, it is also always augmented by an additional gift of grace.

As Aquinas's example illustrates, nature and grace operate in tandem and, in human lived experience, can be difficult to distinguish. Building on the natural human desire for union with God, the gift of grace strengthens, heals, and makes possible that which, while good in itself,

8. Ibid., I-II, q. 109, a. 2.

9. Ibid., I-II, q. 109, a. 3.

10. Stephen J. Duffy, *The Dynamics of Grace: Perspectives in Theological Anthropology*, ed. Peter Phan, New Theology Studies (Collegeville, MN: Liturgical Press, 1993), 127.

is inadequate to fulfilling the desires of God and humanity. This gift is mediated according to the natural human strengths of willing, discoursing, and knowing by means of the senses, so that nature and grace function together for the fulfillment of the human being. Grace is thus not experienced as something which is foreign, but rather something which builds perfectly and seamlessly on the created nature of human beings.

Aquinas's insights have become foundational for subsequent Roman Catholic theology. In building on his structure or rejecting it, other Catholic theologians have generally sought to maintain a sense of the close relationship between nature and grace and the fundamental goodness of the created world. Even when human beings, or other elements of creation, do not achieve their natural potentials in reality, each is possessed of a nature which orients it to achieve its intended end. In some cases, this becomes possible only when the nature is augmented by the grace with which it was designed to function. In the broader picture, the roots of the concept of sacramentality lie in this framework of nature and grace. The claim that all material reality has the potential to mediate the presence of God is grounded both in the recognition of the inherent goodness of the created world and in the insight that grace is mediated according to the natural capacities and strengths of embodied human beings. It is only through the natural that human beings experience and are transformed by the supernatural.

The Biblical Wisdom Tradition

While Aquinas tends to speak in the layered language of Greek philosophy, we find other roots of our contemporary understanding of sacramentality in the Wisdom tradition of the Old Testament. The Wisdom literature is distinctive for its symbolic and personified depictions of God's sustaining interactions with humanity and for its equally practical advice to human beings. In these books the Wisdom that was present at the beginning is directly linked with the Wisdom later offered to humanity in instructive revelation mediated through the created world. The personified figure of Lady Wisdom, present both at creation and throughout human history, provides the symbolic connection between the goodness of creation and the goodness of human flourishing in history. The Wisdom of God is portrayed as the route to such flourishing because of her association with the original goodness of the created world. In the Wisdom literature, as in Aquinas's work, God's grace and human nature function together in the natural desires and pastimes of human beings. Presented to the reader of the Wisdom literature in the contexts of the educational process, in meals, and in Torah study, the figure of Wisdom grounds a sacramental worldview in which God's presence is experienced in the living of a properly ordered human life informed by the intentions of God at creation.

Wisdom and Creation

One of the clear themes in the Wisdom literature is the idea that God created the world with Wisdom. While the precise role of Wisdom is debated, in these creation accounts, Wisdom is described in embodied terms, and is associated with the material tasks of creation. Functioning as a hypostasis of God linking divine transcendence and the material world, Lady Wisdom is portrayed as capable of offering the same wisdom with which the world was created to human beings who seek revelation in history. These credentials ground the sense of sacramentality present in the Wisdom literature's understanding of textual study and meals.

Evoking images of the creation of the world, the Book of Proverbs describes the presence of Wisdom "formed, at the first, before the earth" (Prov 8:23). Here Wisdom speaks in the first person, describing her view of creation, her relationship to God the Creator, and her own role in the event.

> When the earth and the fields were not yet made, nor the first clods of the world. When he established the heavens, there was I, when he marked out the vault over the face of the deep. When he made firm the skies above, when he fixed fast the springs of the deep; When he set for the sea its limit, so that the waters should not transgress his command; When he fixed the foundations of earth, then was I beside him as artisan; I was his delight day by day, playing before him all the while, Playing over the whole of his earth, having my delight with human beings. (Prov 8:26-31)[11]

11. John Collins notes a connection between Wisdom 9:1-2 "where Word *[logos]* and Wisdom are parallel to each other as God's means of creation." Here "the language of emanation or effulgence, however, suggests an even closer connection between Wisdom and the Deity than was envisaged by Sirach." John Collins, *Jewish Wisdom in the Hellenistic Age* (Louisville: Westminister John Knox, 1997), 199. See also Sir 24:3-17; Wis 10:1-2.

In this passage, Wisdom functions as a divine "artisan" who works beside God, contributing to the creative process. Other texts describe the relationship differently, with one stating that Wisdom "leads into the understanding of God, and chooses [God's] works" (Wis 8:4), or that, more than an assistant, Wisdom is best understood as an attribute of God, "a breath of the power of God, and a pure emanation of the glory of the Almighty" (Wis 7:25).[12] Wisdom's presence at creation becomes foundational for understanding the relationship between creation and God's sustaining work in the world. As the Wisdom of Solomon puts it, "She preserved the first-formed father of the world when he alone had been created; And she raised him up from his fall, and gave him power to rule all things" (Wis 10:1-2). Here Wisdom is depicted as the preserver and protector of the first human being. She is also the rescuer from sin (the Fall) and the source of human authority. The text indicates that with Wisdom comes protection, forgiveness, and authority. On the contrary, "when an unrighteous man withdrew from her in his anger, he perished through his fratricidal wrath" (Wis 10:3). This passage and many others in the Wisdom of Solomon and in Sirach attest to the preserving presence of Wisdom throughout salvation history. She is credited with leading the Exodus, "conduct[ing] them by a wondrous road and [becoming] a shelter for them by day a starry flame by night" (Wis 10:17). Her tent is pitched with Israel and "Jerusalem is [her] domain" (Sir 24:8-11). In these texts, the Wisdom literature develops the connection between God's creative and preserving work through the figure of Wisdom.

These texts have many implications for theological understandings of divine revelation in the created world, and thus for the sacramentality of the liturgy as a whole, which emerges out of the context of a graced world. As the sources indicate, Wisdom's insights into the kinds of actions that will lead to human flourishing are gleaned from her deep knowledge and understanding of the created world. The acts of leading the Israelites out of Egypt and through the Red Sea (Wis 10:17-18) or offering advice that will lead to "riches and honor, wealth that endures, and righteousness" (Prov 8:18) are linked by their direct concern for the safety and flourishing

12. See also Sir 24:3, "From the mouth of the Most High I came forth, and covered the earth like a mist."

of humanity. The care offered to the first human, portrayed as alone in a new world, is continued for those who do not "withdraw" from Wisdom.

The causes and effects of Wisdom's relationship with the created world are debated. Some scholars, such as Roland Murphy, suggest that Wisdom's participation in the creation of the world serves as a kind of credential for the instruction she is uniquely equipped to offer to humanity in history.[13] She is able to advise humanity because of her deep knowledge of the way the world was created. Other perspectives suggest that the world itself is revelatory of God only *because* it is orderly and constructed with Wisdom. As John Collins puts it, "[s]ince the world was created with wisdom, it is amenable to understanding. There is an order in creation waiting to be discovered. . . . It underlies the quest for analogies and the predictability of consequence."[14] Emphasizing the connection between the revelatory nature of the world and divine revelation, which comes in other forms, Collins adds that "[t]he self-revelation of creation, however, is in no way opposed to divine revelation. It is the same Wisdom of God that is being revealed in either case."[15] This connection between natural revelation and divine revelation is further developed in Leo Perdue's argument that, "in Job 28, Wisdom is a 'blueprint' for the cosmos, containing its order measurements, and weights, thought known only to the divine artisan."[16] Here Wisdom is herself the divine plan that God consults in the process of creation. Distinct from the "artisan" image of Proverbs, here Wisdom is presented as the organizing structure that holds the world together. To consult Wisdom in history would thus be to consult the governing plan for the created world, operative from the beginning.

Although the texts do not agree on the precise role of Wisdom, their convergence on the relationship between the natural revelation of the created world and the divine Wisdom, which is its source and mediator, points to the presence of God's revelation mediated through creation

13. Roland E. Murphy, *The Tree of Life: An Exploration of Biblical Wisdom Literature*, 3rd ed. (Grand Rapids, MI: Eerdmans, 2002), 118.

14. Collins, *Jewish Wisdom in the Hellenistic Age*, 12.

15. Ibid.

16. Leo G. Perdue, "Cosmology and Social Order in the Wisdom Literature," in *The Sage in Israel and the Ancient Near East*, ed. John G. Gammie and Leo G. Perdue (Winona Lake, IN: Eisenbrauns, 1990), 468.

and human understanding. The personification or hypostasis of Wisdom grounds the categorical pole of God's ongoing offers of revelatory and salvific presence not only in creation but also in history. A close look at the Wisdom tradition indicates that these offers, closely linked to the Wisdom of creation, are frequently, but not exclusively, found in the practices of Torah study and meals.

Wisdom, Word, and Meal

Building on the close association between Wisdom and the creation of the world, the sages of the Wisdom literature, the early rabbis who wrote the *Targumim*, and the Christian evangelists who wrote the Gospels came to understand Wisdom in both revelatory and sacramental terms. Some of these approaches build on the "blueprint" understanding of Wisdom's role in creation, connecting Wisdom to the Torah, and associating the finding of Wisdom with Torah study. Here the revelatory nature of word and text and the revelatory nature of Wisdom are closely linked. Other approaches, less focused on the word, attend to the salvific actions of God in the world. Ranging from the Exodus journey to the wisdom necessary for human flourishing, these approaches focus on the hypostases of God, which are understood to sustain the world in history.

The association between the Wisdom of God and the revelatory word of God in texts and human incarnation begins with the close connection between Wisdom and the Torah in the sapiental literature, and is extended both in the early Jewish *Targumim* and in the first-century Christian understanding of Jesus as the incarnation of Wisdom. In all three cases, Wisdom is associated with the creation and salvation of the world mediated by spoken and written language. In the hymn in praise of Wisdom that begins in Sirach 24, Wisdom, speaking in the first person, reiterates her presence and activity in creation and describes her close relationship to Israel. Her close link with the created world is established in a series of comparisons between Wisdom and trees such as the cedars of Lebanon, the palm trees of Engedi, and the olive trees in the field. Wisdom "bud[s] forth delights like the vine, [her] blossoms are glorious and rich fruit" (Sir 24:17). Following these metaphors drawn from the curricula of the Wisdom schools, which emphasized knowledge of the natural world, we find an innovative identification between Wisdom and Torah. Taking back the narrative, the author of Sirach claims that all that has been said of Wisdom is also "the book of the covenant of the Most High God, the Law which Moses commanded" (Sir 24:23). As Perdue puts it, "the language in Sirach 24 that praises personified Wisdom uses images that refer to the Torah, thus identifying the two."[17] This claim is echoed more precisely in the prophetic Book of Baruch, which states that "she [Wisdom] is the book of the precepts of God, the law that endures forever" (Bar 4:1).[18] The identification of Wisdom and Torah solidifies the relationship between God's revelatory presence in creation and history, and in the text of the Torah. Wisdom can thus become available to humanity both through the natural world and through study of the Torah. According to this argument, the authority of the written word of God is derived from the Wisdom associated with creation.

This connection between text and creation is further solidified in the work of the early rabbis. Referring to the work of Rabbi Hoshaya of Caesarea, Daniel Boyarin notes the claim that God not only consulted Wisdom in the process of creation but also "looked into the Torah as a blueprint in order to create the world."[19] The association of the Torah with the Wisdom hypostasis emphasizes connections between the order of creation and the order of life which is laid out in the Torah. As Collins observes, for Ben Sira as well, "[t]he Torah is the supreme manifestation of wisdom, but wisdom can also be found elsewhere. The law of Sinai is only a concretization of the wisdom implanted in the world at creation."[20] With the Torah understood as the "concretization" of the Wisdom that structures the world, study of the Torah reveals not only the truth about God but also the truth about the inner workings of the world. The one who has Wisdom is close to God and also understands how to flourish in the world.

17. Leo G. Perdue, *Wisdom Literature: A Theological History* (Louisville: Westminster John Knox, 2007), 236. This identification of Torah and Wisdom continues in later Jewish texts and becomes a central theological view of rabbinic Judaism. Perdue, "Cosmology and Social Order in the Wisdom Literature," 236–37. See also Bar 3:9-38 and 4:1-4.

18. See Collins, *Jewish Wisdom in the Hellenistic Age*, 55.

19. Daniel Boyarin, *Border Lines: The Partition of Judaeo-Christianity*, Divinations: Rereading Late Ancient Religion (Philadelphia: University of Pennsylvania Press, 2004), 128.

20. Collins, *Jewish Wisdom in the Hellenistic Age*, 225.

The *Targumim*, the Aramaic translations of the Hebrew Bible which were used in Palestine in antiquity, shed further light on the close association between the Wisdom hypostasis and the word of God offered to humanity in history. In speaking of the significance of the word of God in the context of sacraments and theology of creation, sacramental theologians today have often made the argument that the Hebrew word *davar*, or one of its derivatives, carries the connotation of a word that both describes and effects what it signifies. While contemporary biblical scholarship does not support the claim that *davar* always conveys God's action through speech,[21] it does offer other possibilities for understanding the relationship between word and divine action. The Semitic root *'amr*, which is associated with speaking, is one of these possibilities. In one of its derived forms, *Memra,* which is the Aramaic term for "word," it is sometimes used to signify God's actions on behalf of humanity in the world. This Aramaic term is preserved in the *Targumim*, and in some cases is used to describe a hypostasis of God. In the *Targumim*, the term Memra takes on particular significance both as agent of creation and as mediator between God and humanity. As one Aramaic translation of the first creation narratives describes it, "the Memra of H'[God] said Let there be light and there was light by his Memra."[22] Here the Memra occupies the same role as Wisdom or the logos, acting as agent of creation. The "blueprint" for creation is associated with both Wisdom and Torah, and the agent of creation can be understood as God's word (logos or memra) or as God's Wisdom.

In the *Targumim,* it is also the Memra of God that speaks to humanity and reveals who God is in salvation history. As Boyarin points out, the figure who leads the Israelites through the desert in Exodus 17 is identified in the *Targumim* with the Memra: " 'And the Memra of H' was leading

21. Standing alone, *davar* can have a variety of meanings, ranging from "thing, or matter," to a call to attention. See W. H. Schmidt, "dābhar," in *Theological Dictionary of the Old Testament*, ed. G. Johannes Botterweck and Helmer Ringgren (Grand Rapids, MI: Eerdmans, 1975), 111. While indicative of the prophetic word of revelation, which can indeed be transformative as noted in a previous chapter, *davar* itself is ill equipped to carry the theological weight which has sometimes been assigned to it.

22. Quoted in Boyarin, *Border Lines: The Partition of Judaeo-Christianity*, 119.

them during the day in a pillar of cloud.'"[23] As we saw above, this same task is attributed to Wisdom in the Wisdom of Solomon. Parallel to the Wisdom tradition, especially as it is related to the Torah, the figures of the Memra and the logos, serve to convey the close presence of God in history through word and image, even while they also protect the transcendence of a God who cannot be bound by history.[24]

As we have seen, the terms *Wisdom*, *Logos*, and *Memra* all function to describe the divine hypostasis. These personified depictions of God at work in salvation history for the safety and well-being of the people can be understood in relationship to both the incarnation and the sacramental tradition; they point to the presence of God mediated by material reality in history. The sacramental presentations of Wisdom, Logos, and Memra are foundational for the Christian understanding of the incarnation, which, as Edward Schillebeeckx and others have pointed out, can be understood as the primordial sacrament grounding all others.

The tradition is clear that the presence and effects of Divine Wisdom at work in the world are elusive matters. Who has wisdom? Where can wisdom be found? In some cases, such as in the books of Baruch and Sirach, the biblical authors affirm that Wisdom has come to earth, resides in the Torah, and will remain with humanity. These accounts present a sacramental world view that suggests that the presence of God is to be found in the created world, especially in the sacred texts and in the experiences of human beings. In another, less optimistic tradition, however, the book of Job suggests that only God knows where Wisdom is to be found. Still more pessimistic, the parables of Enoch, a noncanonical text from the first century BCE, refutes the more positive accounts in Sirach

23. In other traditional theophanies, as Boyarin points out, it is also the Memra, rather than an angel or God in person, who speaks with and directs humanity. In Genesis 18:1, where the NAB translates "The Lord appeared to Abraham by the oak of Mamre," the *Targum* states "And was revealed to him [Abraham] the Memra of H." Here it is the Memra to whom visible form is attributed. *Targum* quoted in Daniel Boyarin, "The Gospel of the *Memra:* Jewish Binitarianism and the Prologue to John," *Harvard Theological Review* 94, no. 3 (2001): 257.

24. "In all of the Palestinian Aramaic translations of the Bible, the term *Memra*—as a translation of various terms which in the Hebrew either simply mean God or are names of God—is legion and theologically significant, because these usages parallel nearly exactly the functions of the Logos, as *deuteros theos* in Logos theology." Ibid., 256.

and Baruch, arguing instead that Wisdom did not find a place to dwell with humanity and has withdrawn to heaven (1 Enoch 42:12).[25]

In the traditions in which the figure of Wisdom is described as dwelling with humanity, the ethereal figure associated with creation and found in the Torah is more concretely described in terms associated with female human beings. Ben Sira says that she will meet humanity "like a mother; like a young bride she will receive him" (Sir 15:2). These feminine images mediate the presence of God to humanity in the context of everyday life. Wisdom calls out to human beings (Prov 8:1) to attract their attention. She walks along the heights and at the gates of the city (Prov 8:2-3), pitches her tent (Sir 24:8-10), and has wandered about the earth (Sir 24:6). She claims to "dwell with prudence" (Prov 8:12), and promises flourishing to all who follow her. She brings "glory" and "the blessing of the LORD" to those who hold her fast (Sir 4:13). These human characteristics ground Wisdom in everyday reality. One does not look for her at the ends of the earth but can find her dwelling nearby.

In these local contexts, Wisdom is especially associated with the educational process and with the food which human beings need to nurture and sustain themselves. In many cases, these two themes overlap. In Proverbs, Wisdom invites those most in need of education, the simple and those who lack sense to "eat of my food, and drink of the wine I have mixed" (Prov 9:4-5). Ben Sira associates learning with bread, saying, "Whoever fears the LORD will do this; whoever is practiced in the Law will come to Wisdom . . . She will feed him with the bread of learning, and give him the water of understanding to drink (Sir 15:1, 3). In this reference to the study of the Law, or the Torah, the material elements of bread and water are used to signify the spiritual and educational nourishment which is also provided. Elsewhere Ben Sira compares Wisdom directly to honey[26] and speaks of

25. See Collins, *Jewish Wisdom in the Hellenistic Age*, 51.

26. "You will remember me as sweeter than honey, better to have than the honeycomb" (Sir 24:20). See also: "If you eat honey, my son, because it is good, if pure honey is sweet to your taste, such, you must know, is wisdom to your soul. If you find it, you will have a future, and your hope will not be cut off" (Prov 24:13-14). See also Teresa Berger, *Gender Differences and the Making of Liturgical History: Lifting a Veil on Liturgy's Past* (Burlington, VT: Ashgate, 2011), 70–72.

her fruits.[27] Wisdom is thus depicted as both attractive and sustaining. Found close to home, she shares what is necessary for human flourishing in both the material and the spiritual contexts. As John Collins puts it, "the peculiarity of wisdom is that it is both an attribute of God and an aspect of creation. It is the mode of God's presence in the world, but is also something in which human beings can participate."[28] Human beings not only observe the actions of Wisdom but also participate in her work because, like honey, Wisdom is "sweet" in the short term and because "if you find it, you will have a future, and your hope will not be cut off" (Prov 24:13-14).

While the continued presence or absence of Wisdom was debated among the ancient authors, in the incarnation, Christians find the enfleshing of Wisdom in the person of Jesus of Nazareth as God's decisive commitment to embodied solidarity with human beings in the world.[29] This conviction, grounded in the Wisdom tradition, provides a more symbolic and sacramental presentation of Aquinas's claims about the relationship between nature and grace. As is the case in the sacraments and the incarnation, in the figure of Wisdom, the revelatory presence of God is offered to the simple and those who lack understanding in a manner which is familiar and capable of fostering relationship. For Christians, the incarnation provides the ultimate example both of sacramentality—the claim that the material world has the potential to mediate the presence of God—and the role that language plays in the divine-human relationship. The theological claim that Jesus can be understood as a sacrament is grounded in the incarnation and is closely related to the Wisdom tradition. Read against the backdrop of the Wisdom literature, Jesus' interpretation of the Torah and his focus on human flourishing epitomized by meals, looks back in time toward the Wisdom tradition and forward toward God's enduring care for humanity, in part through the sacraments, in subsequent history.

In the late 1950s, Edward Schillebeeckx was among the first to argue for an understanding of sacrament which expanded the category to include the incarnation. Defining sacrament as "a divine bestowal of salvation

27. "For in cultivating her you will work but little, and soon you will eat her fruit" (Sir 6: 19). "Come to me, all who desire me, and be filled with my fruits" (Sir 24:19).

28. Collins, *Jewish Wisdom in the Hellenistic Age*, 11.

29. For an overview, see Gerald O'Collins, *Christology: A Biblical, Historical, and Systematic Study of Jesus* (Oxford: Oxford University Press, 1995), 37–46.

in an outwardly perceptible form which makes the bestowal manifest; a bestowal of salvation in historical visibility," Schillebeeckx argued that the "the human saving acts of Jesus" both bestow and effect grace in visible form and are thus sacraments.[30] He further suggested that not only are Jesus' actions sacramental but also "the man Jesus, as the personal visible realization of the divine grace of redemption, is *the* sacrament, the primordial sacrament, because this man, the Son of God himself, is intended by the Father to be in his humanity the only way to the actuality of redemption. . . . Human encounter with Jesus is therefore the sacrament of the encounter with God."[31] Read against the background of the Wisdom, Memra, and Logos traditions, the incarnation, while entirely new, can be seen in continuity with the sacramental understanding of God's ongoing presence and visible work in history.

This continuity appears to be in the minds of the evangelists and Pauline writers who occasionally reference the Wisdom tradition with regards to Jesus. In some cases, such as the beginning of the Gospel of John and the Letter to the Colossians, the references are to Wisdom's preexistence with God in the beginning. John begins his Gospel with reference to the role of the logos in creation "in the beginning" (John 1:1) and only subsequently specifies that "the Word became flesh and made his dwelling among us" (John 1:14). The Letter to the Colossians likewise says of Jesus: "He is the image of the invisible God, the firstborn of all creation. For in him were created all things in heaven and on earth, the visible and the invisible, whether thrones or dominions or principalities or powers; all things were created through him and for him. He is before all things, and in him all things hold together. . . . He is the beginning, the firstborn from the dead, that in all things he himself might be preeminent" (Col 1:15-18).[32] The Gospel of Matthew describes Jesus portraying himself as

30. Edward Schillebeeckx, *Christ the Sacrament of the Encounter with God*, 1963 ed. (Franklin, WI: Sheed and Ward, 1999), 15, 17.

31. Ibid., 16.

32. An echo of this can be found in the Nicene Creed, which describes Jesus as "born of the Father before all ages . . . through him all things were made." See the Nicene Creed in "The Liturgy of the Word," in *A Commentary on the Order of Mass of The Roman Missal: A New English Translation*, ed. Edward Foley, et al. (Collegeville, MN: Liturgical Press, 2011), 152–57.

Wisdom when he tells his followers to "Take my yoke upon you and learn from me, for I am meek and humble of heart; and you will find rest for yourselves. For my yoke is easy, and my burden light" (Matt 11:29-30). This can be seen as an echo of Ben Sira's advice regarding Wisdom: "[t]ake her yoke upon your neck; that your mind may receive her teaching. For she is close to those who seek her, and the one who is in earnest finds her" (Sir 51:26).[33] In the case of Jesus, the Word of God takes on the flesh of full humanity, in addition to the human, personal characteristics also evident in the figures of Wisdom and the Memra. In this context, the incarnation moves beyond, yet builds on the previous Wisdom tradition's understanding of divine presence in the world.

When modern-day Christians, gathered for liturgy, listen to the first reading's account of the figure of Wisdom who teaches and sustains humanity, or when they consider the hypostasis of God, symbolized by Wisdom, the logos, or the Memra who creates, appears to, and leads humanity to safety, they are witness to the same strands of sacramental and revelatory interaction present in antiquity. The Wisdom tradition's attention to the close link between creation and human flourishing in history helps to set the context for an understanding of God's presence at creation and in daily events such as meals and study. The suggestion that understanding of the Torah and understanding of the natural world are pursuits oriented toward the same font of God's revelation helps us better understand the relationship between word and sacrament and between liturgical celebration and daily life. When the incarnation of the Logos is considered in this context, it can be seen as a development in the preceding sacramental tradition.

Sacramentality of the World in Twentieth-Century Catholic Theology

While Aquinas's theology and the Biblical context of the Wisdom literature set the historical groundwork for a positive understanding of the relationship between grace and nature, in the twentieth century theologians responded even more directly to a prevailing ecclesiology in which grace

33. See also Elizabeth A. Johnson, *She Who Is: The Mystery of God in Feminist Theological Discourse* (New York: Crossroad, 1992), 156–57.

had come to be associated nearly exclusively with the church. Ecclesiology and sacramental theology were closely linked, since the sacraments had come to be viewed as somewhat isolated instances of grace in an otherwise suspect world. As Karl Rahner put it, in this framework, the sacraments "produce[d] something not otherwise available."[34] Rahner, who was one of the first to respond to this issue, proposed a theory of sacramentality, which approached the liturgy (both word and sacrament) from the perspective of an already graced world. In the final decades of the twentieth century, Louis-Marie Chauvet offered a related theological proposal that considered the sacramentality of language and culture as a framework for theological understanding of the sacraments. Both Rahner and Chauvet intended to address the theological fracture they perceived to exist between word and sacrament. Their theologies of sacramentality help us to consider the Liturgy of the Word and the Liturgy of the Eucharist not only in union with one another but also in union with human culture, language, and the natural world. Such a theology of sacramentality highlights the goodness of human bodies and the natural world around us. It reminds Christians that the liturgical celebration is not only a celebration of our relationship with God but also of the graced relationships between human beings, both as individuals and as peoples, and between humans and the rest of creation.

Rahner's theology of sacramentality is rooted in his understanding of the world as fundamentally graced. Following Aquinas, he writes, "[o]ur actual nature is *never* 'pure' nature. It is a nature installed in a supernatural order which man can never leave, even as a sinner and unbeliever."[35] The reality of this supernatural order indicates that grace is present everywhere. "Grace . . . occurs not only and not even primarily in the sacraments, but wherever a person accepts and realizes in freedom his existence as it is, as radically and immediately dependent on God."[36] Considered in this light, experiences of grace are not confined to the liturgical setting, or even to private prayer. They may occur at any time and

34. Karl Rahner, "On the Theology of Worship," in *Theological Investigations 19* (New York: Crossroad 1983), 142.

35. Karl Rahner, "Nature and Grace," in *Theological Investigations 4* (New York: Crossroad, 1982), 183.

36. Rahner, "On the Theology of Worship," 144.

place in one's daily life. The sacred is not judged as a separate sphere of life, but as intertwined with everyday activities.[37] Just as the Wisdom literature suggests that Wisdom may be found in the experiences of study, meals, and strolling through the streets, Rahner, like Aquinas, argues that the world is fundamentally infused with the presence of God. As the Wisdom of Solomon offers Jewish wisdom to a wider audience, Rahner hoped that his viewpoint might be particularly helpful to those who regard liturgical worship as "a kind of magical procedure [or] as an old-fashioned ritual now devoid of meaning."[38] For such people, Rahner suggests, a theological recognition of the grace found in everyday experiences apart from ritual worship can open a path toward understanding the relationship between religious ritual and everyday life.

In this context, the theological recognition of the world as graced is not only a friendly hand stretched out to those who, for a variety of reasons, may struggle with ritual worship. It is, rather, a fundamental theological statement about the reality of human life, created by and lived in the presence of God. Salvation history and secular history cannot be separated. In the following lengthy but powerful quote, Rahner balances theological respect both for human history as a whole and for the role which God has chosen to play in it.

> The world and its history are the terrible and sublime liturgy, breathing of death and sacrifice, which God celebrates and causes to be celebrated in and through human history in its freedom, this being something which he in turn sustains in grace by his sovereign disposition. In the entire length and breadth of this immense history of birth and death . . . the true liturgy of the world is present—present in such a way that the liturgy which the Son has brought to its absolute fullness on his Cross belongs intrinsically to it, emerges from it, i.e., from the ultimate source of the grace of the world, and constitutes the supreme point of *this* liturgy from which all else draws its life, because everything else is

37. As Nathan Mitchell points out for Rahner, "[h]uman personhood is a *unity*; hence the more I become 'body' the more I become 'spirit'; while the more I become 'spirit' the more I become 'body.' The two are directly (not inversely) proportional." Nathan Mitchell, *Meeting Mystery: Liturgy, Worship, and Sacraments*, ed. Peter C. Phan, Theology in Global Perspective Series (Maryknoll, NY: Orbis Books, 2006), 161.

38. Rahner, "On the Theology of Worship," 148.

> always dependent upon the supreme point as upon its goal and at the same time sustained by it.[39]

The liturgy of the world, as Rahner describes it, is both "terrible and sublime." It is not the polished and sanitary experience that many Christians may associate with Sunday mornings, but is raw with the struggles of birth, death, and sacrifice. It gathers together the whole history of the world, including moments of greatness and moments of terror and must be understood as the context for the more particular Christian liturgies that follow.[40] The Cross, both sublime and terrible, is the moment when the liturgy of the world is brought to its "absolute fullness," and from which the liturgy of the church takes its starting point. While Rahner does not sugarcoat the struggles of human history, he does emphasize the presence of God throughout. Grace is always present, and the grace that emerges most vividly in the liturgy of the church is only present there because it is always already present in the liturgy of the world.

The relationship between the liturgy of the church and the liturgy of the world is thus a close one. Neither serves as a replacement for the other. Drawing on his understanding of symbol, which he defines as "the self-realization of a being in the other, which is constitutive of its essence,"[41] Rahner suggests that the liturgy of the church be understood as "the symbolic presentation of the salvation event which is occurring always and everywhere in the world."[42] Rahner's understanding of symbol, deployed elsewhere to describe the relationship between the Father and the Logos, and between the Sacred Heart of Jesus and the risen Christ,[43] indicates a relationship which makes possible the presence of that which is symbolized. Thus, the liturgy of the church is understood to make present and accessible the liturgy of the world, without which it could not exist. Ecclesial liturgies function as specific and public manifestations

39. Karl Rahner, "Considerations on the Active Role of the Person in the Sacramental Event," in *Theological Investigations 14* (New York: Crossroad, 1983), 169–70.

40. See also Michael Skelley, *The Liturgy of the World: Karl Rahner's Theology of Worship* (Collegeville, MN: Liturgical Press, 1991).

41. Karl Rahner, "The Theology of the Symbol," in *Theological Investigations 4* (New York: Crossroad, 1982), 243.

42. Rahner, "On the Theology of Worship," 146.

43. Rahner, "The Theology of the Symbol."

of grace. They play a vital role as "landmarks"[44] or even "outbursts of the innermost, ever present gracious endowment of the world with God himself into history."[45] Without them, human beings would struggle to recognize the truth that human history contains in itself a preexisting liturgy, which is sustained by God and is swept into what Rahner calls "the banal ordinariness of life."[46] He states,

> Ecclesial worship is important and significant, not because something happens in it that does not happen elsewhere, but because there is present and explicit in it that which makes the world important, since it is everywhere blessed by grace, by faith, hope, and love, and in it there occurred the cross of Christ, which is the culmination of its engraced history and the culmination of the historical explicitness of this history of grace.[47]

That which is implicit in the liturgy of the world is made explicit in the liturgy of the church,[48] creating an ebb and flow between the landmarks of explicit worship and the larger landscape of a graced world.

Within the context of the liturgy of the church, the ritual sacraments play a central role. It is here that God's grace becomes particular to every time and place. Rahner states:

44. Rahner, "Considerations on the Active Role of the Person in the Sacramental Event," in *Theological Investigations 14* (New York: Crossroad, 1983), 169. Rahner is clear that the sacred is not something cut off from the secular world outside. "Rather, in the free breadth of a divine world [humanity] erects a landmark, a sign of the fact that this entire world belongs to God, a sign precisely of the fact that God is adored, experienced, and accepted everywhere as he who, through his 'grace,' has himself set all things free to attain to himself. . . . The sacrament constitutes a small sign, necessary, reasonable and indispensable, within the infinitude of the world as permeated by God. It is the sign which reminds *us* of this limitlessness of the presence of divine grace, and *in this sense* and in no other, precisely in *this particular* kind of anamnesis, is intended to be an event of grace . . . it is a lasting and tragic misunderstanding for us to turn these sacramental signs once more into a circumscribed enclave, such that it is in this alone that God is present, and that the event of his grace takes place."

45. Rahner, "On the Theology of Worship," 143.

46. Ibid., 146.

47. Ibid., 147.

48. Skelley, *The Liturgy of the World*, 101–3.

> This sacramental sign of grace is an effective sign not inasmuch as it would call forth a resolve of God to bestow grace which would not exist without it, but inasmuch as through it precisely this will of God to bestow grace manifests itself at the historical level, and thereby at the same time also renders itself historically irreversible.[49]

Since the ritual sacraments as well as the church itself are connected to realities in the material world (meals, bathing, community gatherings), "the grace which [the sacraments] signify is no abstract grace, but rather the human radicality and the divine depths of those acts in which the fullness of human existence itself is achieved."[50] The sacramental rituals function in a manner similar to Rahner's primordial words, which also serve to express the depths of human existence. Drawing on human words, actions, and gestures, the sacraments include both poetic language and ritual gestures that point to essential human actions such as eating, healing, forgiving, and uniting.

Understood in the context of the liturgy of the world, the sacraments themselves transform those who receive them for the ongoing purposes of God's salvation of the world. In this way, although they are specific to the individual, they also direct the individual away from herself and orient her toward concern for the world. "In the holy sign [the Christian] receives the true body of the Lord in that he knows that this would be useless if he were not in communion with *that* body of God which is the world itself with its destiny, that he is receiving the former body so that in the reality of his own life he may stand in an abiding communion with the latter body."[51] Here sign and causality function together. The sacramental body of Christ is effective as a sign because of its relationship to the presence of God in, but not limited to, the created world. The purpose of this sacramental body is to strengthen the individual Christian's communion not only with her Creator but also with the created world in which she lives. The grace of the sacrament comes not from some point

49. Karl Rahner, "What Is a Sacrament?," in *Theological Investigations 14* (New York: Crossroad, 1983), 144.

50. Karl Rahner, "Introductory Observations on Thomas Aquinas's Theology of the Sacraments in General," in *Theological Investigations 14* (New York: Crossroad, 1983), 156.

51. Rahner, "The Person in the Sacramental Event," 172.

outside the world, but rather is mediated through it "from its heart and center."[52] Once received, it draws the Christian not away from the world, but rather toward it for God's own purposes of salvation. Thus, those in the church "are those who . . . have to make salvation manifest sacramentally to those *others* within the solidarity which embraces all men within a human race which has been redeemed by Christ."[53] The sacraments are both landmarks and causes. They emerge out of the liturgy of the world, but also sustain it.

Rahner's mid-twentieth-century work offered a framework for thinking about the liturgy not as an isolated moment, itself divided into two sections which were unequal in importance, but rather as a particularly concentrated experience of grace which draws its components (words, actions, material realities) from an already graced world and which in turn orients participants back toward the world at large. In the later part of the twentieth century, Louis-Marie Chauvet built on Rahner's insights about the sacramentality of the world by developing a fundamental theology of sacramentality that begins with an understanding of the created world as a gift. Here, the sacraments are also understood as gifts that are transformative and demanding, but that can never be fully possessed. This theology of sacramentality delves deeply into the respect which is due the material elements of the created world. By extension, it also considers human beings within the context of creation and reflects on the obligation the sacraments confer to participate in God's ongoing work in the world.

Chauvet's sacramental theology is simultaneously an argument for the sacramentality of language and the sacramentality of the world. He begins with language, emphasizing it as the clearest example of something which is given, but which can never be bought or even fully possessed. The idea that the world is a revelatory gift, understood according to Chauvet's system of symbolic exchange, indicates that the human response to the world must be one of gratitude and dispossession. This is directly related to the creation of the world by Wisdom and word. "Theologically, the world is confessed as creation insofar as it is marked by the word; and this word makes the world come forth immediately as an offer . . .

52. Ibid., 178.
53. Ibid., 180.

everything is yours; but never forget that all of this is a *gift*."[54] In linking the creation by means of God's word (or Wisdom, or Memra) to his own understanding of language systems which both preexist humanity and demand the participation of individuals in culture, Chauvet makes the argument that the creation of the world is comparable to the beginning of a conversation. Something of great value (which can never be repaid) is offered, and thus the only appropriate action is to respond with tokens of gratitude which, although always unequal to the value of the gift, are sufficient to continue the relationship.

When humanity receives the world from God's speech, therefore, it does not receive a possession. Like language, since language is part of it, creation precedes humanity and provides its context. Relationships with God and with other human beings take place within this context according to the rules of symbolic exchange. "The 'reception' of the world as creation, that is, as 'gift,' implies the 'return-gift' of the offering. Thus, the confession of creation is itself charged with *sacramentality.* It is in the 'sacrament-mystery' of the oblation that the 'mystery' of creation finds its 'expression.' "[55] As noted in chapter 2, the response to God's revelatory gift is always the twin response of gratitude/Eucharist and ethical practice. Chauvet's understanding of the world as gift thus creates two related yet distinct obligations. The first pertains to humanity's treatment of the material elements of the world. The second pertains to the treatment of other human beings who are also seeking a home in the world.

As the traditional Augustinian definition states, "the word is added to the element, and it becomes a sacrament."[56] In the previous chapter, we examined the significance of this "word," which is the fundamental sign. With the help of Chauvet, we now reflect on the significance of the material element. Although the tradition is clear that the material elements themselves function in the sacraments to reveal the presence of God, Chauvet suggests that the use of material elements in the sacraments

54. Louis-Marie Chauvet, *Symbol and Sacrament: A Sacramental Reinterpretation of Christian Existence*, trans. Patrick Madigan and Madeleine Beaumont (Collegeville, MN: Liturgical Press, 1995), 549.

55. Ibid., 551.

56. For an overview of Chauvet's rejection of Augustine's understanding of language, see ibid., 30–34.

can also inversely serve to illuminate the sacred nature of material reality. Sacraments "reveal to us the 'sacramentality' of the world as creation. . . . The most elementary things—water, bread, wine . . . demand 'respect.' . . . Sacraments present the world to us as something we may not use in an arbitrary fashion."[57] In the ritual context Christians are challenged to see the holy in everyday materials such as bread and wine. As Chauvet suggests, these elements themselves are always holy and always bear the possibility of mediating the divine presence. Their very natures are graced, and they may never, even outside the context of ritual, be used "in an arbitrary fashion." As Rahner argued that the sacraments are holy because the world is holy, Chauvet argues that the holiness of the sacraments points to the holiness of creation. In both cases, the relationship between sacraments and creation is clear.

In revealing the sacramentality of creation, the sacraments themselves offer an argument for the human dignity of all. If all created reality is to be treated with respect because of its potential to mediate the presence of God, human beings must be included in this reality. In this way, the sacraments "demand that we make of reality a 'world' for all, and not simply for the well-off."[58] The reception of the sacraments thus imposes a return-gift obligation on the receiver and illuminates the receiver herself as a graced element of the created world. Her holiness signifies the holiness of all other human beings, and creates the obligation to contribute to a world in which the dignity and holiness of every created being is respected.

This obligation is directly connected to the link between the creative power of God's word and the creative power of human language discussed in the previous chapter. Just as human beings both receive language and are obligated in turn to build up language and culture, Chauvet argues that because creation is "linked to the word (of God) . . . it calls humanity to *make a 'world'* out of the universe which it receives, to make throughout history a livable world, that is, a world where each person can find his or her proper place."[59] When the world is received as a gift, the receiver accepts the obligation to offer a return gift of gratitude and to participate in the system of symbolic exchange by accepting the gift, but refraining

57. Ibid., 553.
58. Ibid.
59. Ibid., 550.

from possession of the world. The world must be treated as "an offer, an offering to others, thus to make of it a 'house' open to brothers and sisters where all can find their places."[60]

In accepting the world as an offer, human beings participate in the divine creativity which brought forth the world by Wisdom and word. "Only the human word of creativity can make it cor-respond to the divine word of creation which sets it down as 'ordered'—if it is true that this creative word authoritatively commands chaos to set itself in order so that it may ultimately be hospitable to humankind."[61] As human beings learn to live and flourish in the world, encountering God through word and text, meal and creation, they also participate in God's work of creating and sustaining the world in history. This process of ordering the world in turn has implications for the sacramental celebration. Drawing from the words of both the Wisdom literature of the Old Testament and the body of Christ metaphor of the New Testament, Chauvet observes that

> *Bread cannot become Eucharist under just any condition*. 'Like one who kills a son before his father's eyes is the person who offers a sacrifice from the property of the poor. The bread of the needy is the life of the poor; whoever deprives them of it is a murderer' (Sir 43:24-25). To offer God this bread kneaded from the death of the poor is a sacrilege. To partake of this bread stolen from those who produced it is to eat 'judgment against [oneself]': it is impossible to discern the body of the Lord, namely, this sacramental body where the Head and the members are indissolubly joined together (1 Cor 11:17-34). . . . To pretend to eat the body of Christ unto life, when in fact this bread, taken from the mouths of the poor, is the bearer of death, is to condemn oneself.[62]

The state of creation, for which humans bear some responsibility, thus has direct implications for the celebration of the sacraments. If the created world has not been appropriately received and appreciated as gift, it may be sacramentally impossible to offer the return gift of gratitude to God. The eucharistic return-gift is inadequate if it is not accompanied by the actions of justice and hospitality which contribute to the sacramentality

60. Ibid., 554.
61. Ibid., 553.
62. Ibid., 552. Italics in the original.

of the world. Chauvet concludes: "The theological economy of the sacramental cult is inseparable from the social economy of labor."[63] The liturgy of the church is inseparable from the liturgy of the world.

The twentieth and twenty-first centuries' renewed appreciation for the inherent sacramentality of the world as we experience it has the effect of creating a new context for considering the sacraments and the liturgy itself. The first step in this process is to consider the liturgy of the church in the larger context of a graced world. When the liturgy ceases to be regarded as an isolated, grace-filled hour and is instead seen as a more organic "source" and "summit" of day-to-day life, the holiness and vulnerabilities of material elements, including human bodies, are more clearly understood (see SC 10). These elements, limited yet full of potential, function in both the sacramental economy and the social economy. They both gain and lose their value in these contexts and are more clearly understood as part of the world which is received, but never possessed, as gift.

The second step in the process is to see the sacramentality of the liturgy of the church not only in the eucharistic prayers but also in the liturgy as a whole. When one moves outward from the sacramental elements themselves to consider the sacramentality of the entire liturgical context, one finds grace in the architecture, décor, and even the liturgical books themselves. These books, as Anne Elvey points out, require "plants, animals and human labour" for their production and reproduction.[64] In the liturgical context they may function sacramentally to symbolize both the reality of divine revelation and the complexities of the created world that makes the existence of material texts possible. "The medium of the text (memory, voice, papyrus, paper, digital code) is underscored by complex relationships between text, body, mouth, ear, eye, breath, memory, papyrus, tree, ink, fossils, light, language, persons (ancient or contemporary) who labored to produce the text and the earth that sustained them."[65] As Chauvet suggests, the evidence of God's transformative presence in the bread and wine can point us toward a greater appreciation of the

63. Ibid.

64. Anne Elvey, *The Matter of the Text: Material Engagements Between Luke and the Five Senses* (Sheffield, England: Sheffield Phoenix Press, 2011), 6.

65. Ibid., 16.

sacramentality of other liturgical elements, which are also "fruit of the earth and work of human hands."

Finally, recent work on the concept of sacramentality reminds us that we too are part of the created world. As Aquinas argued, we are created with the potential and the desire to do more than would be possible without the help of grace, yet this embodied potential is still part of creation and is received as a gift every time we encounter another person in relationship. When we receive with gratitude, never seeking to possess the other, we help to build up a world which, even as it "breath[es] of death and sacrifice . . . birth and death,"[66] can also be cocreated with human hands who help to shape it into a world "hospitable to humankind."[67] As created beings, we are both contributors and recipients of this world. As we seek to find our place as Christians, we grow more fully into appreciation and understanding of the sacramentality of the world itself.

Conclusion

"Holy and vulnerable hands." Whether applied to the hands of Jesus or Lady Wisdom, the hands of the eucharistic presider or the hands of the lector on the pages, the hands of the usher with the basket, the hands of the farmer on the wheat, the hands of the picker on the grapes, the hands of the baker in the flour, the hands of the child in the front pew, it is these, our holy and vulnerable bodies, which receive and mediate God's presence in the world. Neither removed from the world nor superior to it, our hands and feet, faces, and voices are transformed into the holy and vulnerable hands of Christ because, like the rest of creation, we too are graced, we too have the potential to participate in the ongoing creation and re-creation of the world. This lens of sacramentality, the perspective that all created reality has the potential to mediate the presence of God, expands our understanding both of the liturgical elements themselves and of the inherent unity of the liturgical action in itself and in relationship to the larger world.

In liturgical jargon, the term "elements" is most often employed to refer to the bread and wine prepared for consecration. The perspective of

66. Rahner, "The Person in the Sacramental Event," 169.

67. Chauvet, *Symbol and Sacrament*, 553.

sacramentality allows us to think more broadly about the sacramentality of material elements. Here we can consider the ways in which the word of God takes material form to mediate God's presence both in the liturgical context and in everyday life. We can first consider the graced materiality of the word of God, offered to us from the holy and vulnerable pens of scribes and tools of bookbinders. Proclaimed by the embodied voice of the reader, we can appreciate the embodied nature of God's word as we experience it. Listening to an Old Testament reading from the Wisdom literature, we are reminded of the ways in which the word of God was offered to humanity in history, both in the words of creation and in the manifestations of the Wisdom, Memra, and logos of God who taught humanity according to the material elements around them. These figures themselves, described in the material terms of trees and food and a light in the darkness leading the Israelites through the desert, remind us that the word of God is always sacramental. It is mediated and embodied, it teaches, transforms, and saves. We ourselves are sometimes the holy and vulnerable mediators of this word as we speak it to one another in the liturgical setting or in a word of hope in our everyday interactions. The lens of sacramentality helps us to look for the mediated and transformative presence of God not only in the consecration of the elements but also in the lectionary readings, in the pews, in the collection baskets, and in the very architecture and elements of the liturgical environment.

In addition to broadening our sense of the sacramentality of the unified liturgy, this perspective also highlights the relationship between the world as it is created and experienced by humanity and the liturgy of the church, which exists as a small, yet significant landmark, or sacrament of God's presence with us. To consider the sacramentality of the world is to accept ourselves as created beings whose efforts to understand the world are also, in effect, efforts to understand God. Success in one will be related to success in the other. Seeking Wisdom through the study of nature, the study of books, the sharing of meals, or through the study, respect, and appreciation of other human beings, can lead us to God in a manner similar to that of the liturgy. While this by no means diminishes the significance of the liturgical celebration or the church as "sign lifted up among the nations" (SC 5), it reminds us of the respect and hospitality which we owe to the rest of creation, and which itself should be celebrated in our liturgies.

The holy and vulnerable nature of the world and of human beings may appear ill equipped to mediate the power and glory of the presence of God. This notion of sacramentality is, however, at the heart of Christian doctrine. It is at the heart of the incarnation, in which, building on the sacramentality of Wisdom, Memra, and Logos, God took on human embodiment, which proved capable of mediating the presence of God in the person of Jesus. Sacramentality is at the heart of the doctrine of the sacraments, which maintain in the face of all opposition, that small bites of food and sips of drink mediate the presence of God for the transformation of human beings and of the world. This perspective is the fundamental unifier both of the liturgy itself and of the liturgy and all that is part of the created world. So familiar as to be overlooked, it provides a lens for deepening our understanding of ourselves, our liturgy, and our world.

chapter 5

Conclusion

The Structure of Unity in Metaphor and Mystery

The image of the "one table of the word of God and Body of Christ" (DV 21) is a metaphor that is simultaneously traditional and yet deeply challenging to contemporary Catholic life and celebration. In engaging this liturgical metaphor, the Second Vatican Council linked the relationship between the Liturgy of the Word and the Liturgy of the Eucharist to broader theological conversations about revelation and sacrament, Scripture and tradition, pneumatology and Christology. These intersections have significant implications for understanding revelation, the "sum total" (DV 2) of which is experienced in the person of Jesus, as well as for the development of a more adequate understanding of the inherent unity of the liturgical celebration. By considering revelation in the context of a liturgical metaphor, the council recognized that it is in the liturgy that Catholic Christians most overtly encounter God's revelatory presence in the proclamation of the Scriptures and the celebration of the sacraments. It is the liturgy as a whole, the Liturgy of the Word and the Liturgy of the Eucharist understood together, which provides the context for a *theologia prima* which shapes who Christians become and what they contribute to the world in which they live.

A fresh look at this liturgy from a variety of theological perspectives illuminates both the unity of the liturgy itself and the depths of the sacramental tradition in which Catholics live their lives, both in and in addition to the liturgy. In this concluding chapter we turn first to *Dei Verbum's* liturgical metaphors, which invite deeper reflection on the relationship between liturgy and divine revelation. We will then turn to a final analysis of the vision of a united liturgy that has emerged from the previous chapters. The final analysis can be understood as an examination of the theological crossbeams, which support the "one table of the word and Body of Christ" (DV 21).

The many liturgical metaphors in *Dei Verbum* invite deeper reflection both on the liturgy itself and on the relationship between liturgy and divine revelation. Offering images in place of canons, these metaphors encourage approaches that expand rather than restrict understanding. Grounded in symbolic rather than mathematical approaches to mystery, they offer a constant reminder of the ineffability of the God who is revealed to humanity in history. This turn to the poetic is especially useful, as Karl Rahner has argued, when dealing with a densely theological topic such as revelation.

A close reading of *Dei Verbum* reveals a plethora of symbols and metaphors. In addition to the many biblical symbols such as mirror (DV 7), storehouse (DV 15), and spouse (DV 23), and the early claim that God "provides constant evidence of himself in created realities" (DV 3), we also find references to liturgical metaphors such as the single "wellspring" or "font" from which Scripture and tradition flow (DV 9), and to the "one table" on which we have focused thus far. These metaphors, as Rahner puts it, "seek to conjure up the Mystery"[1] of which theologies of revelation attempt to speak. The use of symbolic language, rather than the canonical language (including the phrase "let him be anathema"), which was favored by both the Council of Trent and Vatican I, is indicative of a new tone which would be adopted by the Second Vatican Council in response to John XXIII's stated desire to apply "the medicine of mercy rather than that of severity."[2] Concluding that the church must meet "the needs of the present day by demonstrating the validity of her teaching

1. Karl Rahner, "Poetry and the Christian," in *Theological Investigations 4* (New York: Crossroad, 1982), 359.

2. John XXIII, "Gaudet Mater Ecclesia," in *Council Daybook: Vatican II*, ed. Floyd Anderson (National Catholic Welfare Conference, 1962), 27.

rather than by condemnations,"[3] John XXIII set the council on a trajectory of dialogue. Such a choice is, as John O'Malley has recently pointed out, of great significance to the content of the documents. As O'Malley puts it, "[s]tyle, sometimes misunderstood as merely an ornament of speech, an outer garment adorning a thought, is really the ultimate expression of meaning. The 'what' of speech and the 'how' of speech are inseparable."[4] In the case of *Dei Verbum*, the "how" of speech is, in some cases, the use of genres like poetry rather than the canons, which had dominated the texts of relatively recent councils such as Trent and Vatican I.[5] As O'Malley observes, "[a] style choice is an identity choice, a personality choice, a choice in this instance about the kind of institution the council wanted the church to be."[6]

This identity choice becomes evident in a comparison of the ways in which *Dei Verbum* and *Dei Filius*, the First Vatican Council's document on faith and revelation, address the neuralgic issue of the relationship between Scripture and tradition. Quoting nearly directly from the Fourth Session of the Council of Trent, *Dei Filius* states:

> God directed human beings to a supernatural end, that is a sharing in the good things of God that utterly surpasses the understanding of the human mind; *indeed eye has not seen, neither has ear heard, nor has it come into our hearts to conceive what things God has prepared for those who love him (1 Cor 2:9).* Now this supernatural revelation, according to the belief of the universal church, as declared by the Sacred Council of Trent, is contained in written books and unwritten traditions.[7]

Avoiding the infamous "partly . . . partly" formulation by which a draft of the Tridentine text sought to describe the roles of Scripture and tradition in an almost mathematical formulation, this formulation nonetheless

3. Ibid.

4. John O'Malley, *What Happened at Vatican II?* (Cambridge, MA: Harvard University Press, 2010), 306.

5. John O'Malley, "Vatican II: Did Anything Happen?," *Theological Studies* 67, no. 1 (2006): 19–20.

6. O'Malley, *What Happened at Vatican II?*, 305.

7. "Dei Filius," in *Decrees of the Ecumenical Councils*, ed. Norman P. Tanner (Washington, DC: Sheed and Ward, 1990), 806.

describes the revelatory process in fairly prosaic terms. Even the acknowledgment of mystery is stated in a canon: "If anyone says that in divine revelation there are contained no true mysteries properly so-called, but that all the dogmas of the faith can be understood and demonstrated by properly trained reason from natural principles: let him be anathema."[8] In contrast to the style of Vatican I, the Vatican II documents "Sacred tradition and sacred scripture, [which] are bound closely together, and communicate one with the other. Flowing from the same divine wellspring both of them merge, in a sense, and move toward the same goal" (DV 9). Here the image of the font is reminiscent both of the baptismal font by which believers are initiated and of the ancient image, used by Philo, of the word of God flowing like a river into the minds and hearts of believers. The metaphor of the wellspring stimulates the imagination, directing the reader not toward a mathematical division of Scripture and tradition, but toward an image which is constantly in the motion of relationship. Read in tandem with the working title of the schema, *De Fontibus Revelationis*, which would eventually become *Dei Verbum,* the image of the single wellspring or font is an especially strong symbol of unity without clear division or separation.[9] The image of the "one table" (DV 21) draws from the liturgical context as well as from the tradition of the fourth and fifth centuries. The use of this metaphor highlights the human need for physical and spiritual food as well as companionship, opening up the possibilities of relationship between God and humanity, but also between the different "parts" (SC 56) of the liturgy and even the different areas of theology. More multivalent than the "written books and unwritten traditions" of Trent and Vatican I, it too invites theological reflection through the genre of poetry.

In moving toward a more poetic style in the course of the four drafts of *Dei Verbum*, the bishops indicated an ecclesial identity which reflected a

8. Ibid., 811.

9. The Latin plural *fontibus* is indicative of the controversial "two source" theory of revelation which was debated and rejected by the council. For a clear overview of this debate, see Guiseppe Ruggieri, "The First Doctrinal Clash," in *The Formation of the Council's Identity: First Period and Intersession October 1962–September 1963*, ed. Guiseppe Alberigo and Joseph Komonchak, History of Vatican II (Maryknoll, NY: Orbis Books, 1997).

recognition of the realities of mystery and the limits of human language and understanding. The introduction of the poetic and liturgical is especially appropriate in the *Constitution on Divine Revelation* because it is in this document, perhaps more than any other document of the council, that an outline of God's mysterious and revelatory presence is sketched. Rahner, who served on the theological commission that worked on *Dei Verbum,* put it this way: "it is this nameless being [God] that words try to speak when they speak of things that have a name; they try to conjure up the mystery when they indicate the intelligible, they try to summon up infinity when they describe and circumscribe the finite."[10] In the use of metaphors that point beyond themselves to the infinite, *Dei Verbum* suggests a relationship which can never be fully grasped, but which pulls us beyond ourselves. "If God's incomprehensibility does not grip us in a word, if it does not draw us on into his superluminous darkness, if it does not call us out of the little house of our homely, close-hugged truths in to the strangeness of the night that is our real home, we have misunderstood or failed to understand the words of Christianity. For they all speak of the unknown God, who only reveals himself to give himself as the abiding mystery, and to gather home to himself all that is outside himself."[11] Speaking broadly about Christian language, the words of Scripture and poetry, the "Mass of life [and] . . . the Mass of the altar,"[12] Rahner is clear that the words of poetry, the words which human beings use to point toward divine mystery, must call us out of ourselves and out of our comfort zones into the "strangeness of the night that is our real home"—the dazzling night of divine mystery. Metaphors can help in this process because they resist simple equations and do not attempt to circumscribe the path to divine mystery.

Dei Verbum's liturgical metaphors serve as a bookend to the many paragraphs in *Sacrosanctum Concilium* devoted to the important role that divine revelation, particularly as encountered through the Scriptures, plays in the liturgical celebration. The significant role of Scripture is especially clear in *Sacrosanctum Concilium* 6, which grounds liturgical practice in the Scriptures; in paragraph 7, which emphasizes Christ's presence in

10. Rahner, "Poetry and the Christian," 359.

11. Ibid.

12. Ibid., 365.

the liturgical proclamation of the Scriptures; in paragraphs 24 and 35, which discuss the significance of scriptural proclamation and preaching in the liturgy; and in paragraph 121, which suggests that the texts of the church's songs should be drawn from Scripture. The *Constitution on the Sacred Liturgy* also takes up the metaphor of the table, referring to the hope that Christians would be "formed by God's word and be nourished at the table of the Lord's Body (SC 48), and to the "rich fare . . . provided for the faithful at the table of God's word" (SC 51). The close link between the two is emphasized still further in *Sacrosanctum Concilium* 56, which states that "the two parts which in a sense go to make up the Mass, vis. the Liturgy of the Word and the eucharistic liturgy, are so closely connected with each other that they form but one single act of worship" (SC 56).

These metaphors of table and font describe facets of the mystery of divine revelation in terms of material elements most commonly associated with the liturgy. This juxtaposition invites a more imaginative and poetic understanding of the mystery of divine revelation, even as it also expresses the close relationship between God's revelation and the liturgical celebration in which Christians experience the presence of God mediated through material elements including the scriptural and liturgical voices and their own human bodies.

As Christians approach this one table from their various directions, some hearing the voice of the Holy Spirit most clearly in the Eucharist, others in the Scriptures, still others in the sound of the liturgy of the world or in the voices of their brothers and sisters, they are all drawn by a need for nourishment, a need for the bread of life, which is always already offered to them. When this bread comes to them in the words of Scripture, chewed as the scroll consumed by the prophet Ezekiel, or in the sacramental body of Christ broken and shared in the Eucharist, the faithful gather and present themselves and their lives for transformation. The image of the "one table" (DV 21) accepts the mystery of God's revealing presence in the liturgy as well as in the world. It conveys the basic truths that Christians need spiritual food as well as physical food, and that when they come to be fed, they do so as a community gathered around a single table of the word of God and body of Christ. That which is necessary is offered, and although we may not fully understand what we receive, we, nonetheless, as Augustine taught, become it. To move closer to understanding, we must examine both the mystery and our transformed selves.

In the preceding chapters, we have sought to approach the mystery from a variety of angles. The prophetic perspective examined in chapter 1 demonstrated the close connections between prophetic action and sacramental celebration. That chapter examined the symbolic elements of prophecy and the transformative words of the early eucharistic celebrations. In chapter 2 we considered the temptations toward hierarchical dualism, which pairings such as Scripture and sacrament, tradition and Scripture, word and Eucharist, invite. When viewed through the lens of pneumatology, a third point emerges, balancing the equation in a new way by highlighting the unity in relationships of difference. This refocusing of the center displaces individual subjects and invites further reflection on the role of the Holy Spirit in the intersections between concepts, people, and liturgical elements. The third chapter explored the power and potential of language, both human language and the metaphorical use, which is applied to our understanding of God's self-communication. Here we examined intersections in the ways in which language functions in a theology of revelation, in human communications, and in the biblical books. Language is not primarily associated with either "part" of the liturgical celebration, but always precedes the liturgy of the church, shaping human beings even as they in turn shape it. Chapter 4 applied the broadest perspective to the one table. By beginning with the concept of sacramentality, the claim that all created reality is capable of mediating the presence of God, we invited reflection on the unity of the created world and of the close relationship between the created world and the sacramental celebrations. Here the Wisdom literature points toward the goodness of all creation and the function of human flourishing within a graced world.

Each of these perspectives draws us to the table of the bread of life, revealed most fully in the incarnation and sacramentally present to humanity in history. The perspectives, however, like revelation itself, do not divide neatly into categories. Theological reflection on language, for example, intersects in multiple ways with reflection on prophecy, pneumatology, and sacramentality. The unity of the "one table" (DV 21) is more than four edges intersecting only in the corners. It is rather a complex weave of theological themes, which are found throughout the liturgical celebration and which bind it together into one powerful and complex whole. The whole of the liturgy can be approached thematically, as we have done in the previous chapters, but another layer of unity is revealed when the perspectives themselves can be seen to intersect. In the remaining paragraphs we will note some key points of intersection between these perspectives.

We began with a consideration of the way the prophetic lens can illuminate the unity of biblical prophecy and sacramental celebration. The prophetic perspective could also have been considered in the context of a theology of language. Given the broad understanding of language, which David Power defines as "not restricted to the verbal, but refer[ing] to all human media of encounter and exchange, bodily and ritual, as well as verbal,"[13] the prophetic words and actions clearly intersect with the category of language. As Philo points out, the transformative words of the prophets leave an impression on the soul of their hearers. Like a seal set into soft wax, the prophets effect spiritual transformation through their words and gestures. In our contemporary context, this transformation takes place throughout the liturgical celebration whenever the words and actions of Jesus or his fellow prophets are referenced in human language or celebrated in ritual.

The pneumatological perspective is equally inseparable from the perspectives of prophecy and language. From the "double portion" of the Spirit offered to Elisha, to the descent of the Spirit on Jesus at his baptism, to the presence of the Spirit within the earliest Christians who took up their prophetic responsibilities at Pentecost, to the creedal affirmation that the Holy Spirit "has spoken through the prophets,"[14] the intersection between pneumatology and prophecy is clear. This intersection between prophecy and pneumatology emerges from the fact that the prophets stand in the place of difference. As mediators between humanity and God, as well as in the realization of their difference from most other human beings, prophets inhabit what Chauvet calls "the space in the middle."[15] It

13. David N. Power, "Sacrament: Event Eventing," in *A Promise of Presence*, ed. Michael Downey and Richard Fragomeni (Washington, DC: The Pastoral Press, 1992), 59.

14. See the Nicene Creed in "The Liturgy of the Word," in *A Commentary on the Order of Mass of The Roman Missal: A New English Translation*, ed. Edward Foley, et al. (Collegeville, MN: Liturgical Press, 2011), 152–57.

15. Louis-Marie Chauvet, *Symbol and Sacrament: A Sacramental Reinterpretation of Christian Existence*, trans. Patrick Madigan and Madeleine Beaumont (Collegeville, MN: Liturgical Press, 1995), 147.

is here, in this space of difference, which allows for communication, that the Holy Spirit is to be found, creating unity out of difference. In their efforts to restore the relationship between God and humanity, the prophets stand in these points of difference that will become places of unifying encounter. In the liturgical context, the places of unifying intersection between humanity and divinity are also the places of the prophets, whose voices continue to be heard in word and sacrament.

The perspective of language is likewise woven together with the perspectives of pneumatology and sacramentality. As we have seen, the work of the prophets is facilitated by human language broadly understood. It is also the place of the Holy Spirit who is found in the points of difference which make unitive relationship through language possible. When language is considered as the context for human life with God and with one another, it can also be understood in the context of sacramentality. Here we see language as the fundamental mediator of God's grace offered in the form of the word. God's revelatory presence experienced most fully in the incarnation, as well as in Scripture and tradition, comes in the form of the divine self-communication. This divine self-communication is mediated by the created reality of human language. Grace builds on the more familiar nature. The ineffable presence of God is experienced in the familiar contexts of interhuman communication through the visible, aural, and tangible signs we exchange with one another. The perspective of language could easily have been considered through the lens of sacramentality, and the Liturgy of the Eucharist is again seen to be deeply united with the Liturgy of the Word through language, pneumatology, and sacramentality.

Finally, the perspective of sacramentality is inseparable from the other three perspectives as well as woven throughout the whole of the liturgy. In their use of language, for example, the prophets rely on the sacramentality of the created world even as they witness to it. As we have seen, the prophetic words and actions are grounded in everyday life. The invisible reality of divine presence is made visible only through the use of everyday signs drawn from the created world, such as Jeremiah's yoke or pottery. The prophets themselves, with Jesus as the prime example, offer their lives and physical bodies as mediators of God's presence and will for humanity. Even as they draw from the sacramentality of creation to communicate the word of God, the prophetic words and actions also witness to the reality of a graced world in which all people, especially the poor and vulnerable, must be treated with respect. To borrow Chauvet's language, prophets as well as sacraments "demand that we make of reality a 'world' for all, and not simply for the well-off."[16] In their concern for the poor and marginalized the prophets witness to the sacramentality of each human body, which itself is possible only because of the presence of the Holy Spirit sustaining the world. Here all of the perspectives intersect, demonstrating that in history, as well as in the liturgy, the relationship between word of God and body of Christ is one of dynamic and sustained unity.

More than fifty years ago, Yves Congar witnessed the opening of the Second Vatican Council and hoped that there would be a "moment" for the word of God. While the revised lectionary, Catholic Bible studies, and a twenty-first-century pope's concern with the state of Catholic preaching indicate that the church has made great progress in attending to the word of God, there is still much to be done. As we have seen, the unity of the "one table" (DV 21) is not simply a unity between the "two parts" (SC 56) of the Liturgy of the Word and the Liturgy of the Eucharist. It is a complex unity that receives its structure from the many ways, only some of which have been discussed here, in which God's revelatory presence is experienced in history. Considered from this perspective, Yves Congar's concern for a "moment" for the word of God and Pope Francis's recent call for renewal in the realm of Catholic preaching take on even greater urgency. More than a "moment" for the word of God, the twenty-first-century context calls for an integrated approach, one that considers the inherent unity of the "one table" in the context of the liturgy of the world.

This volume has offered one example of such an integrated approach to understanding the theological unity of the liturgy. In so doing, it has relied on three insights central to the maintenance of a unified understanding of revelation and sacrament and the Liturgy of the Word and the Liturgy of the Eucharist. The first of these insights is that the transformative power of God cannot be identified exclusively with either the Liturgy of the Word or the Liturgy of the Eucharist. While many Catholics still associate spiritual transformation nearly exclusively with the sacraments, it is clear that the word of God is also transformative in its prophetic, pneumatological, linguistic, and broadly sacramental contexts. Human beings encounter God

16. Chauvet, *Symbol and Sacrament*, 553.

in particularly public and intense ways in the ritual sacraments, but these encounters do not occur in isolation. The sacramental words are also prophetic words, and the sacraments themselves both mediate and illuminate the presence of God in an already graced world. Spiritual transformation is not derived only from the seven ritual sacraments, but is a possibility in every time and place, including the broader liturgical context.

The second insight is that the word of God and the body of Christ are better understood when they are considered together. While not interchangeable, God's revelatory word and the sacramental body of Christ both convey the bread of life to humanity in history, nourishing them on their spiritual journey. When considered together, it is possible to see the revelatory aspects of the body of Christ and simultaneously to appreciate the sacramental aspects of the word of God. In so doing, we can come to appreciate the material and embodied elements of the word of God as well as the communicative elements, more frequently associated with language, which are also aspects of the body of Christ. We see that while distinct, the two are united in that they form the center of the gathering of Christians seeking the bread of life.

Finally, even as the liturgy itself is one united whole rather than two parts, it is also intimately united with what Rahner calls the liturgy of the world. The language of the liturgy is the language of human life. The sacramentality of the liturgy is the sacramentality of human life. The same Spirit works in both, the same prophetic message is heard in both. While the liturgy of the church is the most overt place of encounter with God, it is also oriented toward the world. This does not detract from the significance of the liturgy of the church, but decentralizes it in a manner which allows for the relationship between God and all of humanity to flourish.

As the memory of the Second Vatican Council is celebrated and the documents continue to be received, the real work of ecumenical and liturgical renewal continues. This work plays out in formal and informal dialogues, in parishes and schools, on the internet and in the embodied liturgical celebration. It is my hope that an integrated understanding of the unity of revelation and sacrament, considered in the liturgical context, can offer new and yet familiar approaches that will move Christians closer to our shared visions of deeper and more unified liturgical celebrations.

Bibliography

Allen, Horace T. "Common Lectionary and Protestant Hymnody: Unity at the Table of the Word—Liturgical and Ecumenical Bookends." In *Liturgical Renewal as a Way to Christian Unity*, edited by James F. Puglisi. Collegeville, MN: Liturgical Press, 2005.

Anderson, E. Byron. "A Body in the Spirit for the World: Eucharist, Epiclesis, and Ethics." *Worship* 85, no. 2 (2011): 98–116.

Aquinas, Thomas. *Summa Theologiae*. New York: Blackfriars and McGraw-Hill, 1963.

Augustine. *Answer to Faustus, A Manichean*. Translated by Roland Teske. Edited by Boniface Ramsey. The Works of St. Augustine: A Translation for the 21st Century. New Rochelle, NY: New City Press, 2007.

———. "The Confessions." In *The Confessions of St. Augustine*. Translated and edited by John K. Ryan. New York: Doubleday, 1960.

———. *De doctrina Christiana*. Translated and edited by R. P. H. Green. New York: Clarendon Press, 1995.

———. *De Trinitate*. Translated by Edmund Hill. Edited by John E. Rotelle. The Works of Saint Augustine: A Translation for the 21st Century. New Rochelle, NY: New City Press, 1991.

———. "Exposition of Psalm 39." In *Expositions of the Psalms 33–50*, 194–223. Translated by Maria Boulding. Edited by John E. Rotelle. The Works of Saint Augustine: A Translation for the 21st Century. New Rochelle, NY: New City Press, 2000.

———. "Exposition on Psalm 40." In *Expositions of the Psalms 33–50*, 224–38. Translated by Maria Boulding. Edited by John E. Rotelle. The Works of Saint Augustine: A Translation for the 21st Century. New Rochelle, NY: New City Press, 2000.

———. "In Answer to the Letters of Petilian, the Donatist." In *Augustin: The Writings Against the Manicheans and Against the Donatists*, 520–628. Translated by J. R. King. Edited by Philip Schaff. Nicene and Post-Nicene Fathers of the Christian Church Part 4. Peabody, MA: Hendrickson, 1995.

———. "Letter 55: Augustine to Januarius." In *Letters 1–99*, 215–36. Translated by Roland Teske. Edited by John E. Rotelle. The Works of Saint Augustine: A Translation for the 21st Century. Brooklyn: New City Press, 2001.

———. *Revisions*. Translated by Boniface Ramsey. Edited by John E. Rotelle. The Works of Saint Augustine: A Translation for the 21st Century. New Rochelle, NY: New City Press, 2010.

———. "Sermon 57." In *Sermons 51-94,* 109–17. Translated by Edmund Hill. Edited by John E. Rotelle. The Works of Saint Augustine: A Translation for the 21st Century. New Rochelle, NY: New City Press, 1991.

———. "Sermon 59." In *Sermons 51-94,* 109–17. Translated by Edmund Hill. Edited by John E. Rotelle. The Works of Saint Augustine: A Translation for the 21st Century. New Rochelle, NY: New City Press, 1991.

———. "Sermon 228B." In *Sermons on the Liturgical Seasons (184–229Z)*, 261–64. Translated by Edmund Hill. Edited by John E. Rotelle. The Works of Saint Augustine: A Translation for the 21st Century. New Rochelle, NY: New City Press, 1993.

———. "Sermon 229: On Holy Easter Sunday about the Sacraments of the Faithful." In *Sermons on the Liturgical Seasons (184–229Z)*, 265–68. Translated by Edmund Hill. Edited by John E. Rotelle. The Works of Saint Augustine: A Translation for the 21st Century. New Rochelle, NY: New City Press, 1993.

———. "Sermon 229A: On Holy Easter Sunday about the Sacraments of the Faithful." In *Sermons on the Liturgical Seasons (184–229Z)*, 269–71. Translated by Edmund Hill. Edited by John E. Rotelle. The Works of Saint Augustine: A Translation for the 21st Century. New Rochelle, NY: New City Press, 1993.

———. *Tractates on the Gospel of John, 55–111*. Translated by John W. Rettig. Edited by Thomas P. Halton. The Fathers of the Church. Washington, DC: CUA Press, 1994.

Baum, Gregory. "A Broadening of the Base: Montreal: Faith and Order." *The Commonweal* 78, no. 19 (August 23, 1963): 505–11.

Beaton, Rhodora. *Embodied Words, Spoken Signs: Sacramentality and the Word in Rahner and Chauvet*. Emerging Scholars Series. Minneapolis, MN: Fortress Press, 2014.

Berger, Teresa. *Gender Differences and the Making of Liturgical History: Lifting a Veil on Liturgy's Past* (Burlington, VT: Ashgate, 2011), 70–72.

Blenkinsopp, Joseph. *A History of Prophecy in Israel*. Revised and Enlarged ed. Louisville: Westminster John Knox, 1996.

Boyarin, Daniel. *Border Lines: The Partition of Judaeo-Christianity*. Divinations: Rereading Late Ancient Religion, edited by Daniel Boyarin, Virginia Burrus, Charlotte Fonrobert, and Robert Gregg. Philadelphia: University of Pennsylvania Press, 2004.

———. "The Gospel of the *Memra:* Jewish Binitarianism and the Prologue to John." *Harvard Theological Review* 94, no. 3 (2001): 243–84.

Bradshaw, Paul. *Eucharistic Origins*. Oxford: Oxford University Press, 2004.

Brown, Raymond. *The Gospel According to John I–XII*. The Anchor Bible, edited by William Foxwell Albright and David Noel Freedman. Vol. 29. Garden City, NY: Doubleday, 1964.

"Canons and Decrees of the Council of Trent." In *Decrees of the Ecumenical Councils*, edited by Norman P. Tanner. Washington, DC: Georgetown University Press, 1990.

Chauvet, Louis-Marie. "Are the Words of the Liturgy Worn Out? What Diagnosis? What Pastoral Approach?" *Worship* 84, no. 1 (2010): 25–37.

———. *The Sacraments: The Word of God at the Mercy of the Body*. Collegeville, MN: Liturgical Press, 2001.

———. *Symbol and Sacrament: A Sacramental Reinterpretation of Christian Existence*. Translated by Patrick Madigan and Madeleine Beaumont. Collegeville, MN: Liturgical Press, 1995.

Chidester, David. *Word and Light: Seeing, Hearing, and Religious Discourse*. Urbana, IL: University of Illinois Press, 1992.

Chupungco, Anscar J. "The Introductory Rites: The ICEL 2010 Translation." In *A Commentary on the Order of Mass of The Roman Missal: A New English Translation*, edited by Edward Foley, et al., 137–41. Collegeville, MN: Liturgical Press, 2011.

Collins, John. *Jewish Wisdom in the Hellenistic Age*. Louisville: Westminster John Knox, 1997.

Congar, Yves. *My Journal of the Council*. Translated by Mary John Ronayne and Mary Cecily Boulding. Collegeville, MN: Liturgical Press, 2012.

Daly, Robert. "Robert Bellarmine and Post-Tridentine Eucharistic Theology." *Theological Studies* 61, no. 2 (2000): 239–60.

"Dei Filius." In *Decrees of the Ecumenical Councils*, edited by Norman P. Tanner. 804–11. Washington, DC: Sheed and Ward, 1990.

"Dei Verbum." In *Vatican Council II: The Basic Sixteen Documents; Constitutions, Decrees, Declarations*. Edited by Austin Flannery. Collegeville, MN: Liturgical Press, 2014.

Duffy, Stephen J. *The Dynamics of Grace: Perspectives in Theological Anthropology*. New Theology Studies. Edited by Peter Phan. Collegeville, MN: Liturgical Press, 1993.

Dulles, Avery. *Models of Revelation*. Maryknoll, NY: Orbis Books, 1992.

———. "The Symbolic Structure of Revelation." *Theological Studies* 41, no. 1 (March 1980): 51–73.

Elvey, Anne. *The Matter of the Text: Material Engagements Between Luke and the Five Senses*. Sheffield, England: Sheffield Phoenix Press, 2011.

"Eucharistic Prayer II." In *A Commentary on the Order of Mass of the Roman Missal: A New English Translation*, edited by Edward Foley, et al. Collegeville, MN: Liturgical Press, 2011.

Foley, Edward, et al., eds. *A Commentary on the Order of Mass of The Roman Missal: A New English Translation*. Collegeville, MN: Liturgical Press, 2011.

Francis. "Evangelii Gaudium." *Origins* 43, no. 27–28 (2013): 421–71.

Gassmann, Günther. *Documentary History of Faith and Order, 1963–1993*. Faith and Order Paper no. 159, Geneva: WCC Publications, 1993.

Gray, Mark M., Mary L. Gautier, and Melissa A. Cidade. "Views from the Pews: Parishioner Evaluations of Parish Life in the United States." National Association for Lay Ministry; Emerging Models of Pastoral Leadership Project, 2013.

Grootaers, Jan. "Ebb and Flow Between Two Seasons." In *The Formation of the Council's Identity First Period and Intersession October 1962–September 1963*, edited by Guiseppe Alberigo and Joseph A. Komonchak. History of Vatican II, Volume 2, 515–64. Maryknoll, NY: Orbis Books, 1997.

Hilkert, Mary Catherine. *Naming Grace: Preaching and the Sacramental Imagination*. New York: Continuum, 1997.

Hill, William. *Search for the Absent God: Tradition and Modernity in Religious Understanding*. New York: Crossroad, 1992.

Hooker, Morna. *The Signs of a Prophet: The Prophetic Actions of Jesus*. Harrisburg, PA: Trinity Press International, 1997.

Irwin, Kevin W. *Context and Text: Method in Liturgical Theology*. Collegeville, MN: Liturgical Press, 1994.

———. "The *petit* Chauvet on the Sacraments." *Antiphon* 6, no. 3 (2001): 49–54.

Jeffery, Peter. *Translating Tradition: A Chant Historian Reads* Liturgiam Authenticam. Collegeville, MN: Liturgical Press, 2005.

John XXIII. "Gaudet Mater Ecclesia." In *Council Daybook: Vatican II*, edited by Floyd Anderson. 25–29: National Catholic Welfare Conference, 1962.

Johnson, Elizabeth A. *Ask the Beasts: Darwin and the God of Love*. New York: Bloomsbury, 2014.

———. *She Who Is: The Mystery of God in Feminist Theological Discourse*. New York: Crossroad, 1992.

Johnson, Luke Timothy. *Prophetic Jesus, Prophetic Church: the Challenge of Luke-Acts to Contemporary Christians*. Grand Rapids, MI: Eerdmans, 2011.

Jungmann, Josef Andreas. "Constitution on the Sacred Liturgy." In *Commentary on the Documents of Vatican II*. Volume 1. Translated by Lalit Adolphus. Edited by Herbert Vorgrimler. New York: Herder and Herder, 1967.

Kasper, Walter. *Jesus the Christ*. Mahwah, NJ: Paulist Press, 1976.

Kilmartin, Edward. *The Eucharist in the West: History and Theology*. Collegeville, MN: Liturgical Press, 1998.

Lennan, Richard. "The Church as a Sacrament of Hope." *Theological Studies* 72, no. 2 (2011): 247–74.

"The Liturgy of the Word." In *A Commentary on the Order of Mass of The Roman Missal: A New English Translation*, edited by Edward Foley, et al., 152–59. Collegeville, MN: Liturgical Press, 2011.

"Lumen Gentium." In *Vatican Council II: The Basic Sixteen Documents; Constitutions, Decrees, Declarations*. Edited by Austin Flannery. Collegeville, MN: Liturgical Press, 2014.

Marion, Jean-Luc. *God Without Being: Hors-texte*. Translated by Thomas A. Carlson. Chicago: University of Chicago Press, 1991.

Markus, R. A. *Signs and Meanings: World and Text in Ancient Christianity*. Liverpool: Liverpool University Press, 1996.

McBrien, Richard P. "Sacramentality, principle of." In *The HarperCollins Encyclopedia of Catholicism*, edited by Richard P. McBrien. San Francisco: HarperCollins, 1995.

McDermott, John M. "The Christologies of Karl Rahner." *Gregorianum* 67 (1986): 87–123.

McKenna, John H. "Eucharistic Epiclesis: Myopia or Microcosm?" *Theological Studies* 36, no. 2 (1975): 265–84.

———. "Eucharistic Presence: An Invitation to Dialogue." *Theological Studies* 60, no. 2 (1999): 294–317.

McWilliam, Joanne. "Weaving the Strands Together: A Decade in Augustine's Eucharistic Theology." In *Collectanea Augustiniana: Mélanges T. J. van Bavel*, edited by Mathijs Lamberigts, Bernard Bruning, and J. van Houtem, 497–506. Louvain: Leuven University Press, 1990.

Meier, John P. *A Marginal Jew: Rethinking the Historical Jesus*. The Anchor Bible Reference Library, edited by David Noel Freedman. Volume Two: *Mentor, Message, and Miracles*. New York: Doubleday, 1994.

———. *A Marginal Jew: Rethinking the Historical Jesus*. The Anchor Bible Reference Library, edited by David Noel Freedman. Volume Three: *Companions and Competitors*. New York: Doubleday, 2001.

Mitchell, Nathan. "But Only Say the Word." *Worship* 80, no. 5 (2006): 453–66.

———. *Meeting Mystery: Liturgy, Worship, and Sacraments*. Theology in Global Perspective Series. Edited by Peter C. Phan. Maryknoll, NY: Orbis Books, 2006.

———. "Mystery and Manners: Eucharist in Post-Modern Theology." *Worship* 79, no. 2 (2005): 131–51.

———. "Sacrament: More Than Meets the Eye." *Worship* 83, no. 4 (2009): 350–65.

Moltmann, Jürgen. *The Crucified God: The Cross of Christ as the Foundation and Criticism of Christian Theology*. Minneapolis, MN: Fortress Press, 1993.

Morgan, Edward. *The Incarnation of the Word: The Theology of Language of Augustine of Hippo*. London: T&T Clark, 2011.

Murphy, Roland E. *The Tree of Life: An Exploration of Biblical Wisdom Literature*. 3rd ed. Grand Rapids, MI: Eerdmans, 2002.

Niehoff, Maren R. "What Is in a Name? Philo's Mystical Philosophy of Language." *Jewish Studies Quarterly* 2, no. 2 (1995): 220–52.

O'Collins, Gerald. *Christology: A Biblical, Historical, and Systematic Study of Jesus*. Oxford: Oxford University Press, 1995.

O'Malley, John. *What Happened at Vatican II?*: Cambridge, MA: Harvard University Press, 2010.

———. "Vatican II: Did Anything Happen?" *Theological Studies* 67, no. 1 (2006): 3–33.

Organ, Deborah A. "Enkindling Fire in and among Us: An Operative Theology of Liturgical Preaching." *Liturgical Ministry* 15 (Winter 2006): 10–17.

Oxford English Dictionary. Oxford, England: Oxford University Press, 2012.

Perdue, Leo G. "Cosmology and Social Order in the Wisdom Literature." In *The Sage in Israel and the Ancient Near East*, edited by John G. Gammie and Leo G. Perdue. Winona Lake, IN: Eisenbrauns, 1990.

———. *Wisdom Literature: A Theological History*. Louisville: Westminster John Knox, 2007.

Philo. "Allegorical Interpretation." In *The Works of Philo: Complete and Unabridged.* Translated by Charles Duke Yonge. Peabody, MA: Hendrickson, 1993.

———. "On Dreams." In *The Works of Philo: Complete and Unabridged.* Translated by Charles Duke Yonge. Peabody, MA: Hendrickson, 1993.

———. "On the Creation of the World." In *The Works of Philo: Complete and Unabridged.* Translated by Charles Duke Yonge. Peabody, MA: Hendrickson, 1993.

———. "On the Decalogue." In *The Works of Philo: Complete and Unabridged.* Translated by Charles Duke Yonge. Peabody, MA: Hendrickson, 1993.

———. "On the Migration of Abraham." In *The Works of Philo: Complete and Unabridged.* Translated by Charles Duke Yonge. Peabody, MA: Hendrickson, 1993.

———. "On the Posterity of Cain." In *The Works of Philo: Complete and Unabridged.* Translated by Charles Duke Yonge. Peabody, MA: Hendrickson, 1993.

———. "On the Sacrifices of Cain and Abel." In *The Works of Philo: Complete and Unabridged.* Translated by Charles Duke Yonge. Peabody, MA: Hendrickson, 1993.

———. "Questions and Answers on Genesis." In *The Works of Philo: Complete and Unabridged*. Translated by Charles Duke Yonge. Peabody, MA: Hendrickson, 1993.

———. "That the Worse Attacks the Better." In *The Works of Philo: Complete and Unabridged*. Translated by Charles Duke Yonge. Peabody, MA: Hendrickson, 1993.

Power, David N. "A Prophetic Eucharist in a Prophetic Church." In *Eucharist: Toward the Third Millennium*, 27–50. Chicago: Liturgical Training Publications, 2007.

———. "Sacrament: Event Eventing." In *A Promise of Presence*, edited by Michael Downey and Richard Fragomeni, 271–99. Washington, DC: The Pastoral Press, 1992.

———. *Sacrament: The Language of God's Giving*. New York: Crossroad, 1999.

———. "The Word in the Liturgy: Incarnating the Gospel in Cultures." In *Sacraments: Revelation of the Humanity of God: Engaging the Fundamental Theology of Louis-Marie Chauvet*, edited by Phillippe Bordeyne and Bruce T. Morrill, 47–61. Collegeville, MN: Liturgical Press, 2008.

Rahner, Karl. "Considerations on the Active Role of the Person in the Sacramental Event." Translated by David Bourke. In *Theological Investigations 14*, 161–84. New York: Crossroad, 1983.

———. "Faith and Sacrament." Translated by Joseph Donceel and Hugh M Riley. In *Theological Investigations 23*, 181–88. New York: Crossroad, 1983.

———. *Foundations of Christian Faith: An Introduction to the Idea of Christianity*. Translated by William V. Dych. New York: Crossroad, 1997.

———. *Hearer of the Word: Laying the Foundation for a Philosophy of Religion*. Translated by Joseph Donceel. Edited by Andrew Tallon. New York: Continuum, 1994.

———. "Introductory Observations on Thomas Aquinas's Theology of the Sacraments in General." Translated by David Bourke. In *Theological Investigations 14*, 149–85. New York: Crossroad, 1983.

———. "Nature and Grace." Translated by Kevin Smyth. In *Theological Investigations 4*, 165–88. New York: Crossroad, 1982.

———. "On the Theology of Worship." In *Theological Investigations 19*, 141–49. New York: Crossroad, 1983.

———. "Poetry and the Christian." Translated by Kevin Smyth. In *Theological Investigations 4*, 357–67. New York: Crossroad, 1982.

———. "Priest and Poet." Translated by Karl H. Kruger and Boniface Kruger. In *Theological Investigations 3*, 294–317. New York: Crossroad, 1982.

———. "The Theology of the Symbol." Translated by Kevin Smyth. In *Theological Investigations 4*, 221–52. New York: Crossroad, 1982.

———. "What Is a Sacrament?" Translated by David Bourke. In *Theological Investigations 14*, 135–48. New York: Crossroad, 1983.

———. "The Word and the Eucharist." Translated by Kevin Smyth. In *Theological Investigations 4*. 253–86. New York: Crossroad, 1982.

Ratzinger, Joseph. "Commentary on *Dei Verbum*." In *Commentary on the Documents of Vatican II*. Translated by Lalit Adolphus. Edited by Herbert Vorgrimler. Volume 3. New York: Herder and Herder, 1969.

Regan, Patrick. "Quenching the Spirit: The Epiclesis in Recent Roman Documents." *Worship* 79, no. 5 (2005): 386–404.

Robson, James. *Word and Spirit in Ezekiel*. Library of Hebrew Bible/Old Testament Studies. Edited by Claudia Camp and Andrew Mein. New York: T&T Clark, 2006.

Rodger, Patrick C., and Regin Prenter, J. Russell Chandran, Joseph Sittler. *Paper 39. Report of the Theological Commission on Worship*. Geneva: World Council of Churches, Commission on Faith and Order, 1963.

Ruggieri, Guiseppe. "The First Doctrinal Clash." In *The Formation of the Council's Identity: First Period and Intersession October 1962–September 1963*, edited by Guiseppe Alberigo and Joseph Komonchak, 231–66. *History of Vatican II*. Maryknoll, NY: Orbis Books, 1997.

Runia, David. *Philo in Early Christian Literature: A Survey*. Jewish Traditions in Early Christian Literature. Minneapolis, MN: Fortress Press, 1993.

"Sacrosanctum Concilium." In *Vatican Council II: The Basic Sixteen Documents; Constitutions, Decrees, Declarations*. Edited by Austin Flannery. Collegeville, MN: Liturgical Press, 2014.

Satterlee, Craig Alan. *Ambrose of Milan's Method of Mystagogical Preaching*. Collegeville, MN: Liturgical Press, 2002.

Savon, Hervé. *Saint Ambrose devant L'Exégèse de Philon le Juif*. Paris: Études Augustiniennes, 1977.

Schillebeeckx, Edward. *Christ the Sacrament of the Encounter with God*. 1963 ed. Franklin, WI: Sheed and Ward, 1999.

Schmidt, W. H. "dābhar." Translated by John T. Willis and Geoffrey W. Bromiley. In *Theological Dictionary of the Old Testament*, edited by G. Johannes Botterweck and Helmer Ringgren, 84–124. Grand Rapids, MI: Eerdmans, 1975.

Schneiders, Sandra M. *The Revelatory Text: Interpreting the New Testament as Sacred Scripture*. 2nd ed. Collegeville, MN: Liturgical Press, 1999.

———. *Women and the Word: The Gender of God in the New Testament and the Spirituality of Women*. New York: Paulist Press, 1986.

Semmelroth, Otto. *The Preaching Word: On the Theology of Proclamation*. New York: Herder and Herder, 1965.

Serra, Dominic E. "The Introductory Rite: Theology of the Latin Text and Rite." In *A Commentary on the Order of Mass of The Roman Missal: A New English*

Translation, edited by Edward Foley, et al., 125–32. Collegeville, MN: Liturgical Press, 2011.

Skelley, Michael. *The Liturgy of the World: Karl Rahner's Theology of Worship*. Collegeville, MN: Liturgical Press, 1991.

Stacey, W. David. "The Lord's Supper as Prophetic Drama: The A. S. Peake Memorial Lecture, 1993." *Epworth Review* 21, no. 1 (January 1994): 65–74.

———. *Prophetic Drama in the Old Testament*. London: Epworth Press, 1990.

Taft, Robert. "From Logos to Spirit: On the Early History of the Epiclesis." In *Gratias Agamus: Studien zum eucharistischen Hochgebet*, edited by Andreas Heinz and Heinrich Rennings, 489–502. Freiburg: Herder, 1992.

Tobin, Thomas. "The Prologue of John and Hellenistic Jewish Speculation." *Catholic Biblical Quarterly* 52 (1990): 252–69.

Townshend, Robert Todd. *The Sacramentality of Preaching: Homiletic Uses of Louis-Marie Chauvet's Theology of Sacramentality*. American University Studies. New York: Peter Lang, 2009.

Wawrykow, Joseph. "Grace." In *The Theology of Thomas Aquinas*, edited by Rik Van Nieuwenhove and Joseph Wawrykow, 192–221. Notre Dame, IN: University of Notre Dame Press, 2005.

Weaver, Rebecca. "Prayer." In *Augustine Through the Ages*, edited by Allan D. Fitzgerald. Grand Rapids, MI: Eerdmans, 1999.

Winston, David. *Logos and Mystical Theology in Philo of Alexandria*. Cincinnati: Hebrew Union College Press, 1985.

———. "Philo's Linguistic Theory." In *Heirs of the Septuagint: Philo, Hellenistic Judaism and Early Christianity; Festschrift for Earl Hilgert*, edited by David Runia, David Hay, and David Winston, 109–25. Brown Judaic Studies. The Studia Philonica Annual III, Atlanta: Scholar's Press, 1991.

World Council of Churches. *The Report of the Theological Commission on Tradition and Traditions. Fourth World Conference on Faith and Order, Montreal, Canada, 12–26 July, 1963*. Faith and Order Paper no. 40. Geneva: World Council of Churches, Faith and Order Commission, 1963.

Zheltov, Michael. "The Moment of Eucharistic Consecration in Byzantine Thought." In *Issues in Eucharistic Praying in East and West: Essays in Liturgical and Theological Analysis*, edited by Maxwell Johnson, 263–306. Collegeville, MN: Liturgical Press, 2011.

Index

Fifty years ago, *Dei Verbum* called Catholics to reflect on the inherent unity of the "one table of the word of God and the body of Christ." Drawing from a variety of ancient and modern insights, the author proposes a fresh view of word and sacrament as interrelated facets of God's one enduring revelation. Like a table with four sides, the unity of the Liturgy of the Word and the Liturgy of the Eucharist can be seen from the viewpoints of prophecy, pneumatology, language, and sacramentality.

Grounded in Catholic systematic theology, the author extends the conversation to ecumenical reflection and implications for communities of faith.

Rhodora E. Beaton, PhD, is assistant professor of systematic theology at St. Catherine University and specializes in sacraments, liturgy, and theology of revelation. She is the author of *Embodied Words, Spoken Signs: Sacramentality and the Word in Rahner and Chauvet.*

ISBN 978-0-8146-8056-8

51995

9 780814 680568

U.S. $19.95